1000 GERMAN SENTENCES:
Dual Language German-English Interlinear & Parallel Text

GERMAN BOOKS AND AUDIO BY L2 PRESS

GERMAN SHORT STORIES: Dual Language German-English, Interlinear & Parallel Text

GERMAN GRAMMAR BY EXAMPLE: Dual Language German-English, Interlinear & Parallel Text

1000 GERMAN SENTENCES: Dual Language German-English, Interlinear & Parallel Text

This series of three books provides over 5000 sentences of interlinear + parallel text plus audio for maximum comprehension of every word and sentence.

1000 GERMAN SENTENCES:
Dual Language German-English
Interlinear & Parallel Text

Copyright © 2020 by Aron Levin

All Rights Reserved. No part of this book, or associated audio files, may be reproduced, stored in a retrieval system, or transmitted, in any form or by any means, electronic, mechanical, photocopying, recording, internet usage, or otherwise, without the prior written permission from the publisher.

ISBN 978-1-952161-04-9

www.L2Press.com

First Edition

Table of contents

Introduction	i
Alphabet and Pronunciation	iii
1000 Sentences	1

Introduction

DEAR LANGUAGE LEARNER: This book is intended for beginner and intermediate learners of German who want to improve their German vocabulary, grammar, speaking, and listening abilities through massive exposure to one thousand wide-ranging sentences.

The examples are presented in an *interlinear + parallel text* format for maximum comprehension of every aspect of the sentence. On the left side of the page is the interlinear German, phonetic notation, and translation. Linguistically speaking, this is an interlinear gloss containing three lines of interlinear text: (1) the first line is the German source text; (2) the second line is the phonetic notation using the International Phonetic Alphabet (IPA), which improves speaking and provides a better overall understanding of the word; and (3) the third line is the English translation of the German word(s) directly above. On the right side of the page is the parallel text, which is an English translation of the German sentence. The translation style of the parallel text is a free translation, whereas the third line of the interlinear gloss is essentially a literal translation.

A German audio file recorded by a professional voice actor is available as a companion to this book (available for purchase at L2Press.com). Audio files are important for developing correct pronunciation and listening ability. The second line of the interlinear is an excellent pronunciation guide, but there is no replacement for trying to emulate the pronunciation of a native speaker when it comes to developing a good accent.

How To Use This Book

Mastering the meaning, pronunciation, and usage of every sentence in this book will tremendously improve your German reading and speaking proficiency. Once you deeply understand this wide swath of German vocabulary and sentence structures, all future German-learning endeavors will be much more fruitful, reading native German materials will be far easier, and your speaking and listening abilities will be greatly enhanced. How does one master all of the material in this book? Here are tips to get you started:

1. *Extensive and Intensive reading.* Intensive reading is a way of reading a small amount of text in a detailed manner with the goal of understanding as much as possible while extracting new vocabulary and grammar. Extensive reading is reading quickly, for pleasure, without looking up anything, for as long as you want, with the goal of gaining massive exposure to the language.

   This book allows language learners at any stage to easily perform both intensive and extensive reading. If you want to improve your speaking abilities, then read aloud. If you aren't sure of the correct pronunciation, then look at the line below for immediate feedback and correction. And if you don't know the meaning of the word, look at the third line for immediate feedback and correction of the meaning. If you don't understand the meaning of a phrase or sentence, then look at the parallel text. This constant cycle of instant feedback and correction is a key attribute of deliberate practice and will accelerate your learning like never before.

2. *Active listening.* Written text with a corresponding audio file is a powerful combination of language learning tools. By hearing the language spoken, you can appreciate and imitate the prosody, melody, and intonation of the language. Combined, the audio and phonetic notation will instill confidence, consistency, and clarity in how the language is spoken.

Introduction

Prioritize active listening, which requires all of your attention and concentration, over passive listening, which requires little effort and yields minimal results. Productive active listening exercises include:

- *Shadowing*: listen to audio while repeating it nearly simultaneously, directly following the sound like a shadow. Ideally do this both with and without looking at a written version of the audio. Try to speak, as best as you can, like the native speaker, focusing on vowel sounds, vowel length, new consonant sounds, stress, and intonation.
- *Repeating*: listen to audio and then pause to repeat. Like shadowing, ideally do this both with and without looking at a written version of the audio, and try to mimic the native speaker as closely as possible. This technique, along with shadowing, is useful for developing a good accent.
- *Listening-Reading*: listen to German audio while reading English text. Following along in English while listening to German audio helps you understand what is being said. Can also combine this technique with shadowing (Listen to German, shadow in German, read English). This technique is great for developing your ability to understand spoken German.
- *Transcribing*: listen to an audio file while pausing frequently to write down exactly what you heard. Correct your transcription against the original text. This technique is good for *focused* listening comprehension.

3. *Spaced repetition with chunks.* Spaced repetition software (SRS) is an electronic flashcard system with a built-in algorithm that shows you the cards at optimal times for memorizing. If you are having trouble remembering certain words, phrases, and sentences after reading them many times, and you like to review flashcards, then put them into an SRS, such as Anki or Memrise, and review daily. "Chunks" are groups of two or more words that you should learn as a single unit. Chunks give you vocabulary, context, and grammar all in a short phrase. As an example, take the simple sentence "Last night I ate dinner with my family." Instead of breaking up the sentence into eight individual words and learning them all separately, it would be far more productive to learn it in three chunks - "last night", "I ate dinner", and "with my family". Now you know three chunks of words that work together and can be applied in new situations. "I was at my friend's house *last night*", "*I ate dinner* already", "I'm visiting New York *with my family*". Intuiting the grammar through context is more enjoyable and useful than laboring through tedious grammar exercises.

4. *Converse with a speaking partner.* In parallel to mastering the content of this book using the above techniques, find a native speaker and converse with them on a consistent basis, preferably at least one hour per week. The ideal practice partner is patient and will not simply correct your errors but will prompt you to self-correct. If you desire to speak fluently, there is no substitute for conversation practice.

Special notes about the German

1. Arrows are used in the third line of the interlinear to indicate separable verbs, passive voice, and several *Perfekt* verb tenses. See the *German Grammar By Example* book for more on these topics.

2. Exclamation marks (!) are used in the third line of the interlinear to translate words that are used as "emphasis particles". See the *German Grammar By Example* book for a more comprehensive description with examples.

Alphabet and Pronunciation

The German Alphabet and Pronunciation		
Letter[1]	IPA[2]	Similar sound in English[3]
A, a	/ɑː/	f<u>a</u>ther
B, b	/beː/	<u>b</u>oy / to<u>p</u> (at end of word)
C, c	/tseː/	ha<u>ts</u> / <u>c</u>at
D, d	/deː/	<u>d</u>og / ha<u>t</u> (at end of word)
E, e	/eː/	f<u>a</u>te / g<u>e</u>t
F, f	/ɛf/	<u>f</u>ind
G, g	/geː/	<u>g</u>et
H, h	/hɑː/	<u>h</u>elp
I, i	/iː/	j<u>ea</u>ns / s<u>i</u>t
J, j	/jot/	<u>y</u>ear
K, k	/kɑː/	<u>k</u>ite
L, l	/ɛl/	<u>l</u>ip
M, m	/ɛm/	<u>m</u>other
N, n	/ɛn/	<u>n</u>ever
O, o	/oː/	h<u>o</u>pe / h<u>o</u>t
P, p	/peː/	<u>p</u>et
Q, q	/kuː/	always "qu" which makes /kv/ sound
R, r	/ɛʀ/	guttural R / open *a* at end of word
S, s	/ɛs/	<u>s</u>and / <u>z</u>oo
T, t	/teː/	<u>t</u>oe
U, u	/uː/	sp<u>oo</u>n / p<u>u</u>t
V, v	/faʊ/	<u>f</u>ind
W, w	/veː/	<u>v</u>ibe
X, x	/ɪks/	ki<u>ck</u>s
Y, y	/ʏpsɪlon/	like U with pursed lips
Z, z	/tsɛt/	ha<u>ts</u>
Ä, ä	/ɛː/	b<u>e</u>d
Ö, ö	/øː/	b<u>ir</u>d (New Zealand pronunciation)
Ü, ü	/yː/	like U with pursed lips
ß	/ɛs tsɛt/	<u>s</u>and

(1) The first column lists the German letters in alphabetical order, including the three umlauts and Eszett.
(2) The second column shows the phonemic notation for each German letter as described by the International Phonetic Alphabet (IPA).
(3) The third and final column lists English words with comparable consonant and vowel sounds. The relevant sound is underlined.

1000 Sentences

(1) Große Hochzeiten mit vielen Gästen sind bei uns Tradition.
ˈgʁoːsə ˈhɔxtsaɪtn mɪt ˈfiːlən ˈgɛstən zɪnt baɪ ʊns tʁadiˈtsioːn
big weddings with many guests they are with us tradition

A big wedding with many people is our tradition.

(2) Eine Flasche Mineralwasser mit zwei Gläsern bitte.
ˈaɪnə ˈflaʃə mineˈʁaːlˌvasɐ mɪt tsvaɪ ˈglɛːzɐn ˈbɪtə
a bottle mineral water with two glasses please

A bottle of mineral water and two glasses please.

(3) Nebenan wohnt eine Familie mit drei Kindern.
neːbnˈan ˈvoːnt ˈaɪnə faˈmiːliə mɪt dʁaɪ ˈkɪndɐn
next door it lives a family with three children

A family with three children lives next door.

(4) Einer meiner Freunde ist Koch in einem schicken Restaurant.
ˈaɪnɐ ˈmaɪnɐ ˈfʁɔɪndə ɪst kɔx ɪn ˈaɪnəm ˈʃɪkn ʁɛstoˈʁɑ̃ː
one of my friends he is chef in a fancy restaurant

A friend of mine is a chef at a fancy restaurant.

(5) Eine gesunde Ernährung ist wichtig, wenn man lange
ˈaɪnə gəˈzʊndə ɛɐˈnɛːʁʊŋ ɪst ˈvɪçtɪç vɛn man ˈlaŋə
a healthy diet it is important if one long

leben will.
ˈleːbn vɪl
he wants to live

A healthy diet is important if you want to live a long time.

(6) Kommt ein Pferd in eine Bar, sagt der Barkeeper: »Was
kɔmt aɪn pfeːɐt ɪn ˈaɪnə baːɐ zaːkt deːɐ ˈbaːɐˌkiːpɐ vas
it comes a horse into a bar he says the bartender what

ziehst du so ein langes Gesicht?«
tsiːst duː zoː aɪn ˈlaŋəs gəˈzɪçt
you pull you such a long face

A horse walks into a bar, and the bartender asks, "Why the long face?".

(7) Ein bisschen Sport ist ja gesund, aber man soll es nicht
aɪn ˈbɪsçən ʃpɔʁt ɪst jaː gəˈzʊnt ˈaːbɐ man zɔl ɛs nɪçt
a little exercise it is ! healthy but one one should it not

übertreiben.
yːbɐˈtʁaɪbn
to overdo

A little exercise is healthy, but you should not overdo it.

(8) Ein Mechaniker repariert mein Auto.
aɪn meˈçaːnɪkɐ ʁepaˈʁiːɐt maɪn ˈaʊto
a mechanic he fixes my car

A mechanic is fixing my car.

(9) Hier wird ein neues Einkaufszentrum gebaut.
hiːɐ vɪʁt aɪn ˈnɔɪəs ˈaɪnkaʊfsˌtsɛntʁʊm gəˈbaʊt
here → a new shopping center ← it is being built

A new shopping center is being built here.

(10) **Über meinem Schreibtisch hängt ein Bild von meinen Kindern.**
ˈyːbɐ ˈmaɪnəm ˈʃʁaɪpˌtɪʃ ˈhɛŋt aɪn bɪlt fɔn ˈmaɪnən ˈkɪndɐn
above my desk it hangs a picture of my children

A picture of my children is hanging above my desk.

(11) **Einer aktuellen Studie zufolge nimmt die Umweltverschmutzung zu.**
ˈaɪnɐ aktuˈɛlən ˈʃtuːdiə tsuˈfɔlgə nɪmt diː ˈʊmvɛltfɛɐˌʃmʊtsʊŋ tsuː
a recent study according to it increases→ the pollution ←

A recent study shows that pollution is still increasing.

(12) **Auf unserer Hochzeit spielte eine kleine Band.**
aʊf ˈʊnzəʁɐ ˈhoːxtsaɪt ˈʃpiːltə ˈaɪnə ˈklaɪnə bant
at our wedding it played a small band

A small band played at our wedding.

(13) **Laut der Wettervorhersage wird es morgen regnen.**
laʊt deːɐ ˈvɛtɐfoːɐˌheːɐzaːgə vɪʁt ɛs ˈmɔʁgn̩ ˈʁeːgnən
according to the weather forecast it will it tomorrow to rain

According to the weather forecast, it will rain tomorrow.

(14) **Opioidabhängigkeit ist ein großes Problem.**
opioˈiːtˈapˌhɛŋɪçkaɪt ɪst aɪn ˈgʁoːsəs pʁoˈbleːm
opioid addiction it is a big problem

Addiction to opioids is a big problem.

(15) **Erwachsene müssen zahlen, doch Kinder haben freien Eintritt.**
ɛɐˈvaksənə ˈmʏsn̩ ˈtsaːlən dɔx ˈkɪndɐ ˈhaːbn̩ ˈfʁaɪən ˈaɪnˌtʁɪt
adults they must to pay but kids they have free entry

Adults must pay, but admission is free for kids.

(16) **Nach der ersten Halbzeit führt unsere Mannschaft 2 zu 0.**
naːx deːɐ ˈeːɐstən ˈhalptsaɪt fyːɐt ˈʊnzəʁə ˈmanʃaft tsvaɪ tsuː nʊl
after the first half it leads our team two to zero

After the first half, our team leads 2-0.

(17) **Nach dem Essen gab es ein leckeres Dessert.**
naːx deːm ˈɛsn̩ gaːp ɛs aɪn ˈlɛkəʁəs dɛˈseːɐ
after the meal there was a delicious dessert

After the meal there was a delicious dessert.

(18) **Nach dem Essen gingen wir spazieren.**
naːx deːm ˈɛsn̩ ˈgɪŋən viːɐ ʃpaˈtsiːʁən
after the meal we went for a walk→ we ←

After we ate, we went for a walk.

(19) **Ahmed ist hierhergekommen, um Englisch zu studieren.**
ˈaxmɛt ɪst ˈhiːɐˈheːɐgəˌkɔmən ʊm ˈɛŋlɪʃ tsuː ʃtuˈdiːʁən
Ahmed he came here in order to→ English ← to study

Ahmed came here to study English.

(20) **Alle Gruppenmitglieder waren bei der Sitzung anwesend.**
'alə 'gʁʊpnmɪtˌgliːdɐ 'vaːʁən baɪ deːɐ 'zɪtsʊŋ 'anˌveːzənt
all group members they were at the meeting present

All group members were present at the meeting.

(21) **Die ganzen Proteste haben nichts bewirkt.**
diː 'gantsən pʁoˈtɛstə 'haːbn nɪçts bəˈvɪʁkt
the entire protests → nothing ← they achieved

All the protests achieved nothing.

(22) **Wenn man nicht zur Beerdigung anderer Leute geht,**
vɛn man nɪçt tsuːɐ bəˈeːɐdɪgʊŋ 'andəʁɐ 'lɔɪtə geːt
if one not to the funeral of other people one goes

werden sie auch nicht zur eigenen kommen.
'veːɐdn ziː aʊx nɪçt tsuːɐ 'aɪgənən 'kɔmən
they will they also not to your own to come

Always go to other people's funerals, otherwise they won't come to yours.

(23) **Sonst noch was? – Nein, das ist alles.**
zɔnst nɔx vas naɪn daːs ɪst 'aləs
else anything else no that it is all

Anything else? - No, that's all.

(24) **Ist vom Abendessen noch was übrig?**
ɪst fɔm 'aːbntˌɛsn nɔx vas 'yːbʁɪç
it is from the dinner anything else remaining

Are there any leftovers from dinner?

(25) **Nehmen wir den Bus oder die U-Bahn?**
'neːmən viːɐ deːn bʊs 'oːdɐ diː 'uːˌbaːn
we take we the bus or the subway

Are we going by bus or subway?

(26) **Gehen wir heute Abend aus?**
'geːən viːɐ 'hɔɪtə 'aːbnt aʊs
we go out→ we tonight ←

Are we going out tonight?

(27) **Treffen wir uns nach wie vor um halb neun?**
'tʁɛfn viːɐ ʊns naːx viː foːɐ ʊm halp nɔɪn
we meet still at half nine

Are we still meeting at half past eight?

(28) **Kommst du? – Ja, klar!**
kɔmst duː jaː klaːɐ
you come you yes of course

Are you coming? - Of course!

(29) **Habt ihr diesen Sommer etwas Besonderes vor? – Keine**
haːpt iːɐ 'diːzən 'zɔmɐ 'ɛtvas bəˈzɔndəʁəs foːɐ 'kaɪnə
you plan→ you this summer anything special ← no

Ahnung, wir haben noch nichts geplant.
'aːnʊŋ viːɐ 'haːbn nɔx nɪçts gəˈplaːnt
idea we → still nothing ←we have planned

Are you doing anything special this summer? - I don't know, we don't have any plans yet.

(30) **Sind Sie für oder gegen das öffentliche Rauchverbot? – Ich**
zɪnt ziː fyːɐ 'oːdɐ 'geːgn daːs 'œfntlɪçə 'ʁaʊxfɛɐˌboːt ɪç
you are you for or against the public smoking ban I

bin dafür.
bɪn daˈfyːɐ
I am for it

Are you for or against a ban on smoking in public? - I am for it.

(31) **Zahlen Sie bar? Sie können auch mit EC-Karte bezahlen.**
ˈtsaːlən ziː baːɐ ziː ˈkœnən aʊx mɪt eˈtseːˌkaʁtə bəˈtsaːlən
you pay you cash you you can also with debit card to pay

Are you paying with cash? You can also pay by debit card.

(32) **Bist du sicher, dass die Bibliothek heute geöffnet ist? Ich dachte, sie wäre geschlossen.**
bɪst duː ˈzɪçɐ das diː biblioˈteːk ˈhɔɪtə ɡəˈœfnət ɪst ɪç
you are you sure that the library today open it is I
ˈdaxtə ziː ˈvɛːʁə ɡəˈʃlɔsn̩
I thought it it was closed

Are you sure that the library is open today? I thought it was closed.

(33) **Hast du dich gut ausgeruht? Wir haben einen anstrengenden Tag vor uns.**
hast duː dɪç ɡuːt ˈaʊsɡəˌʁuːt viːɐ ˈhaːbn̩ ˈaɪnən
→ well ←you have rested we we have a
ˈanʃtʁɛŋəndn̩ taːk foːɐ ʊns
taxing day ahead of us

Are you well rested? We have a busy day ahead of us.

(34) **Sobald ich den Hochzeitstermin weiß, sage ich dir Bescheid.**
zoˈbalt ɪç deːn ˈhɔxˌtsaɪtstɛʁˈmiːn vaɪs ˈzaːɡə ɪç
as soon as I the wedding date I know I let you know→ I
diːɐ bəˈʃaɪt
←

As soon as I know the date of the wedding, I'll let you know.

(35) **Bei uns zuhause gibt es oft scharfes Essen.**
baɪ ʊns tsuˈhaʊzə ˈɡiːpt ɛs ɔft ˈʃaʁfəs ˈɛsn̩
at our home there is often spicy food

At home we often eat spicy food.

(36) **Unser Betrieb stellt Möbel wie Sofas und Tische her.**
ˈʊnzɐ bəˈtʁiːp ʃtɛlt ˈmøːbl̩ viː ˈzoːfas ʊnt ˈtɪʃə
our company it manufactures→ furniture like couches and tables
heːɐ
←

At our company we make home furniture like couches and tables.

(37) **Im Augenblick sind keine Tische frei.**
ɪm ˈaʊɡn̩ˌblɪk zɪnt ˈkaɪnə ˈtɪʃə fʁaɪ
at the moment there are no tables available

At the moment there are no tables available.

(38) **Im Zoo gibt es 34 verschiedene Vogelarten.**
ɪm tsoː ˈɡiːpt ɛs fiːɐʊntˈdʁaɪsɪç fɛɐˈʃiːdənə ˈfoːɡl̩ˌaːɐtn̩
at the zoo there are thirty-four different bird species

At the zoo they have 34 different species of birds.

(39) **Sei leise. Die Kinder schlafen schon.**
zaɪ ˈlaɪzə diː ˈkɪndɐ ˈʃlaːfn̩ ʃoːn
be quiet the kids they sleep already

Be quiet. The kids are already sleeping.

(40) **Bevor wir auf die Party gehen, will ich mir etwas Hübscheres anziehen.**
bəˈfoːɐ viːɐ aʊf diː ˈpaːɐti ˈgeːən vɪl ɪç miːɐ ˈɛtvas ˈhʏpʃəɐəs ˈanˌtsiːən
before we to the party we go I want I → something nicer ←to put on

Before we go to the party, I want to change into a nicer outfit.

(41) **Das Fahrradfahren ist auf dem Gehweg verboten.**
das ˈfaːɐʁaːtˌfaːʁən ɪst aʊf deːm ˈgeːˌveːk fɛɐˈboːtn
the bicycling it is on the sidewalk forbidden

Biking on the sidewalk is not allowed.

(42) **Guten Appetit! / Lasst es euch schmecken!**
ˈguːtən apeˈtiːt last ɛs ɔɪç ˈʃmɛkn
good appetite let it to you to taste good

Bon appétit! / Enjoy your meal!

(43) **Meine beiden Kinder haben braune Augen.**
ˈmaɪnə ˈbaɪdn ˈkɪndɐ ˈhaːbn ˈbʁaʊnə ˈaʊgən
my both children they have brown eyes

Both of my children have brown eyes.

(44) **Die Giro- und Sparkonten sind kostenlos.**
diː ˈʒiːʁo ʊnt ˈʃpaːɐˌkɔntn zɪnt ˈkɔstnloːs
the checking and savings accounts they are free

Both the checking and savings accounts are free.

(45) **Tschüss. Bis bald!**
tʃʏs bɪs balt
bye until soon

Bye. See you soon!

(46) **Rufen Sie im Notfall diese Nummer an.**
ˈʁuːfn ziː ɪm ˈnoːtˌfal ˈdiːzə ˈnʊmɐ an
call→ in case of emergency this number ←

Call this number in case of emergency.

(47) **Beruhige dich bitte. Alles ist in Ordnung.**
bəˈʁuːɪgə dɪç ˈbɪtə ˈaləs ɪst ɪn ˈɔʁdnʊŋ
calm down please everything it is okay

Calm down, please. Everything is okay.

(48) **Wer kann den Weltmeister schlagen?**
veːɐ kan deːn ˈvɛltˌmaɪstɐ ˈʃlaːgn
who he can the world champion to beat

Can anyone beat the world champion?

(49) **Kann ich mir mal deine Zahnbürste ausleihen? – Nein, das wäre ja ekelhaft!**
kan ɪç miːɐ maːl ˈdaɪnə ˈtsaːnbʏʁstə ˈaʊsˌlaɪən naɪn daːs ˈvɛːʁə jaː ˈeːkəlhaft
I can I to me ! your toothbrush to borrow no that it would be ! disgusting

Can I borrow your toothbrush? - No, that's disgusting!

(50) **Kann ich noch eine Decke haben? Mir ist kalt.**
kan ɪç nɔx ˈaɪnə ˈdɛkə ˈhaːbn miːɐ ɪst kalt
I can I another blanket to have to me it is cold

Can I get another blanket? I'm cold.

(51) Könnte ich bitte sofort einen Termin bekommen? –
ˈkœntə ɪç ˈbɪtə zoˈfɔʁt ˈaɪnən tɛʁˈmiːn bəˈkɔmən
I could I please immediately an appointment to get
Das ist leider nicht möglich.
das ɪst ˈlaɪdɐ nɪçt ˈmøːklɪç
that it is unfortunately not possible

Can I have an appointment immediately? - Unfortunately that is not possible.

(52) Kann ich per Kreditkarte bezahlen?
kan ɪç pɛʁ kʁeˈdiːtˌkaʁtə bəˈtsaːlən
I can I by credit card to pay

Can I pay by credit card?

(53) Darf ich das auf deinem Drucker ausdrucken?
daʁf ɪç daːs aʊf ˈdaɪnəm ˈdʁʊkɐ ˈaʊsˌdʁʊkn
I may I this on your printer to print

Can I print this on your printer?

(54) Kann ich kurz mit dir sprechen?
kan ɪç kʊʁts mɪt diːʁ ˈʃpʁɛçn
I can I briefly with you to talk

Can I talk to you briefly?

(55) Kannst du mich später nochmal anrufen? Wir essen gerade.
kanst duː mɪç ˈʃpɛːtɐ ˈnɔxˌmaːl ˈanˌʁuːfn viːʁ ˈɛsn gəˈʁaːdə
you can you me later again to call we we eat right now

Can you call me again later? We are eating right now.

(56) Kannst du mir mal helfen? Ich kann die Kiste nicht allein
kanst duː miːʁ maːl ˈhɛlfn ɪç kan diː ˈkɪstə nɪçt aˈlaɪn
you can you me ! to help I I can the box not alone
heben.
ˈheːbn
to lift

Can you help me? I can't lift the box alone.

(57) Kannst du Opa dabei helfen, seinen neuen Computer
kanst duː ˈoːpa daˈbaɪ ˈhɛlfn ˈzaɪnən ˈnɔɪən kɔmˈpjuːtɐ
you can you grandpa with it to help his new computer
einzurichten?
ˈaɪntsuˌʁɪçtn
to set up

Can you help your grandpa set up his new computer?

(58) Kannst du mir bis morgen früh Bescheid sagen?
kanst duː miːʁ bɪs ˈmɔʁgn fʁyː bəˈʃaɪt ˈzaːgn
you can you me by tomorrow morning to let (someone) know

Can you let me know by tomorrow morning?

(59) Könntest du bitte ein bisschen lauter sprechen?
ˈkœntəst duː ˈbɪtə aɪn ˈbɪsçən ˈlaʊtɐ ˈʃpʁɛçn
you could you please a little louder to speak

Can you please speak a little louder?

(60) Machst du bitte mal das Licht an? Ich kann nichts sehen.
maxst duː ˈbɪtə maːl daːs lɪçt an ɪç kan nɪçts ˈzeːən
you turn on→ you please ! the light ← I I can nothing to see

Can you please turn on the light? I can't see anything.

(61) Kannst du heute mit dem Hund zum Tierarzt gehen?
kanst duː ˈhɔɪtə mɪt deːm hʊnt tsʊm ˈtiːʁˌaʁtst ˈgeːən
you can you today with the dog to the veterinarian to go

Can you take the dog to the vet today?

(62) **Kannst du mal bitte die Lautstärke herunterdrehen?**
kanst du maːl ˈbɪtə diː ˈlaʊtˌʃtɛʁkə hɛˈʁʊntɐˌdʁeːən
you can you ! please the volume to turn down

Can you turn down the volume, please?

(63) **Carola gibt viel Geld für ihre Hobbys aus.**
kaˈʁola ɡɪpt fiːl ɡɛlt fyːɐ ˈiːʁə ˈhɔbis aʊs
Carola she spends→ a lot of money for her hobbies ←

Carola spends a lot of money on her hobbies.

(64) **Vorsicht! Der Boden ist nass.**
ˈfoːɐˌzɪçt deːɐ ˈboːdn ɪst nas
caution the floor it is wet

Caution! The floor is wet.

(65) **Kinder hängen finanziell von ihren Eltern ab.**
ˈkɪndɐ ˈhɛŋən finanˈtsiɛl fɔn ˈiːʁən ˈɛltɐn ap
children they depend→ financially on their parents ←

Children are financially dependent on their parents.

(66) **Kinder über zehn Jahren müssen den vollen Eintrittspreis bezahlen.**
ˈkɪndɐ ˈyːbɐ tseːn ˈjaːʁən ˈmʏsn deːn ˈfɔlən ˈaɪntʁɪtsˌpʁaɪs bəˈtsaːlən
children over ten years they have to the full entry price to pay

Children over 10 years old pay the full entrance fee.

(67) **Der Unterricht fällt nächste Woche aus.**
deːɐ ˈʊntɐˌʁɪçt fɛlt ˈnɛçstə ˈvɔxə aʊs
the class it is canceled→ next week ←

Class is canceled next week.

(68) **Kaffee oder Tee? – Ich hätte lieber Tee.**
ˈkafe ˈoːdɐ teː ɪç ˈhɛtə ˈliːbɐ teː
coffee or tea I I would prefer tea

Coffee or tea? - I would prefer tea.

(69) **Komm her, ich muss dir etwas zeigen.**
kɔm heːɐ ɪç mʊs diːɐ ˈɛtvas ˈtsaɪɡn
come here I I have to you something to show

Come here so that I can show you something.

(70) **Komm rein, die Tür ist offen.**
kɔm ʁaɪn diː tyːɐ ɪst ˈɔfn
come in the door it is open

Come in, the door is open.

(71) **Komm, wir setzen uns auf die Bank dort drüben.**
kɔm viːɐ ˈzɛtsn ʊns aʊf diː baŋk dɔʁt ˈdʁyːbn
come we we sit on the bench over there

Come, we'll sit on that bench over there.

(72) **Glückwunsch zur Geburt deiner Tochter.**
ˈɡlʏkˌvʊnʃ tsuːɐ ɡəˈbuːɐt ˈdaɪnɐ ˈtɔxtɐ
congratulations to the birth of your daughter

Congratulations on the birth of your daughter.

(73) **Könntest du später nochmal anrufen?**
ˈkœntəst duː ˈʃpɛːtɐ ˈnɔxˌmaːl ˈanˌʁuːfn
you could you later again to call

Could you call again later?

(74) **Könntest du mir mal ein Beispiel geben?**
ˈkœntəst duː miːɐ maːl aɪn ˈbaɪʃpiːl ˈgeːbn
you could you me ! an example to give

Could you give me an example?

(75) **Eine Zwiebel klein schneiden und zusammen mit dem Fleisch braten.**
ˈaɪnə ˈtsviːbl klaɪn ˈʃnaɪdn ʊnt tsuˈzamən mɪt deːm
an onion small to cut and together with the
flaɪʃ ˈbʁaːtn
meat to fry

Cut an onion into small pieces and fry it together with the meat.

(76) **Papa, kannst du mir bei den Hausaufgaben helfen?**
ˈpaːpa kanst duː miːɐ baɪ deːn ˈhaʊsaʊfˌgaːbn ˈhɛlfn
dad you can you me with the homework to help

Dad, can you help me with my homework?

(77) **Der Alltag kann manchmal langweilig werden.**
deːɐ ˈalˌtaːk kan ˈmançmaːl ˈlaŋvaɪlɪç ˈveːɐdn
the daily life it can sometimes boring to become

Day-to-day life is sometimes boring.

(78) **Trotz meiner Grippe ging ich zur Arbeit, was eine schreckliche Idee war.**
tʁɔts ˈmaɪnɐ ˈgʁɪpə gɪŋ ɪç tsuːɐ ˈaʁbaɪt vas ˈaɪnə
despite my flu I went I to work what a
ˈʃʁɛklɪçə iˈdeː vaːɐ
terrible idea it was

Despite having the flu, I went to work, which was a terrible idea.

(79) **Hat irgendjemand den Unfall mit angesehen?**
hat ˈɪʁgntˌjeːmant deːn ˈʊnfal mɪt ˈangəˌzeːən
→ anyone the accident ←he witnessed

Did anyone witness the accident?

(80) **Bist du zu Fuß oder mit dem Fahrrad gekommen?**
bɪst duː tsuː fuːs ˈoːdɐ mɪt deːm ˈfaːɐˌʁaːt gəˈkɔmən
→ you by foot or with the bicycle ←you came

Did you come by foot or bike?

(81) **Hat dir das Essen geschmeckt?**
hat diːɐ daːs ˈɛsn gəˈʃmɛkt
→ the meal ←you enjoyed

Did you enjoy your meal?

(82) **Bist du mit dem Auto gekommen? – Nein, zu Fuß.**
bɪst duː mɪt deːm ˈaʊto gəˈkɔmən naɪn tsuː fuːs
→ you with the car ←you came no by foot

Did you get here by car? - No, I walked.

(83) **Hast du gut geschlafen?**
hast duː guːt gəˈʃlaːfn
→ you well ←you slept

Did you sleep well?

(84) **Hast du das Geschenk für deine Mutter eingepackt?**
hast duː daːs gəˈʃɛŋk fyːɐ ˈdaɪnə ˈmʊtɐ ˈaɪngəˌpakt
→ you the gift for your mother ←you wrapped

Did you wrap your mother's gift?

(85) **Das Abendessen ist fast fertig.**
das ˈaːbntˌɛsn ɪst fast ˈfɛɐtɪç
the dinner it is almost ready

Dinner is nearly ready.

(86) **Die Brausetablette in Wasser auflösen, nicht zerkauen.**
diː ˈbʁaʊzətaˌblɛtə ɪn ˈvasɐ ˈaʊfˌløːzn nɪçt tsɛɐ̯ˈkaʊən
the fizzy tablet in water to dissolve not to chew

Dissolve the tablet in water, don't chew it.

(87) **Essen Affen wirklich Bananen, oder ist das nur ein Mythos?**
ˈɛsn ˈafən ˈvɪʁklɪç baˈnaːnən ˈoːdɐ ɪst daːs nuːɐ̯ aɪn ˈmyːtɔs
they eat monkeys actually bananas or it is that just a myth

Do monkeys actually like to eat bananas, or is that just a myth?

(88) **Glaube nicht immer, was man dir sagt. Oft ist es nur gelogen.**
ˈɡlaʊbə nɪçt ˈɪmɐ vas man diːɐ̯ ˈzaːkt ɔft ɪst ɛs nuːɐ̯ ɡəˈloːɡn
believe not always what one to you he says often it is it only a lie

Do not believe everything you are told. It is often a lie.

(89) **Geh bei roter Ampel nicht über die Straße. Das ist gefährlich.**
ɡeː baɪ ˈʁoːtɐ ˈampl nɪçt ˈyːbɐ diː ˈʃtʁaːsə das ɪst ɡəˈfɛːɐ̯lɪç
go at red light not across the street that it is dangerous

Do not cross the street while the light is red. That is dangerous.

(90) **Essen Vegetarier auch Eier?**
ˈɛsn veɡeˈtaːʁiɐ aʊx ˈaɪɐ
they eat vegetarians also eggs

Do vegetarians eat eggs?

(91) **Glaubst du an Gott?**
ɡlaʊpst duː an ɡɔt
you believe you in God

Do you believe in God?

(92) **Hast du eine Creme für trockene Haut?**
hast duː ˈaɪnə kʁɛːm fyːɐ̯ ˈtʁɔkənə haʊt
you have you a cream for dry skin

Do you have a cream for dry skin?

(93) **Hast du schon den Führerschein?**
hast duː ʃoːn deːn ˈfyːʁɐʃaɪn
you have you yet the driver's license

Do you have a driver's license yet?

(94) **Hast du eine Leiter, die ich mir ausleihen könnte? Ich will die Fenster putzen.**
hast duː ˈaɪnə ˈlaɪtɐ diː ɪç miːɐ̯ ˈaʊsˌlaɪən ˈkœntə ɪç vɪl diː ˈfɛnstɐ ˈpʊtsn
you have you a ladder that I I could borrow I I want the windows to clean

Do you have a ladder I can borrow? I want to clean the windows.

(95) **Hast du eine Blumenvase?**
hast duː ˈaɪnə ˈbluːmənˌvaːzə
you have you a flower vase

Do you have a vase for the flowers?

(96) Hast du alle nötigen Zutaten fürs Abendessen?
hast duː ˈalə ˈnøːtɪgn ˈtsuːtaːtn fyːɐs ˈaːbntˌɛsn
you have you all necessary ingredients for the dinner

Do you have all the ingredients necessary to make dinner?

(97) Hast du einen Regenschirm bei dir, falls es regnet?
hast duː ˈaɪnən ˈʁeːgnʃɪʁm baɪ diːɐ fals ɛs ˈʁeːgnət
you have you an umbrella with you in case it rains

Do you have an umbrella with you in case it rains?

(98) Kannst du mir ein Buch empfehlen?
kanst duː miːɐ aɪn buːx ɛmˈpfeːlən
you can you to me a book to recommend

Do you have any book recommendations?

(99) Hast du Kleingeld für den Automaten? Ich habe nur
hast duː ˈklaɪnˌgɛlt fyːɐ deːn aʊtoˈmaːtən ɪç ˈhaːbə nuːɐ
you have you coins for the machine I I have only

Scheine.
ˈʃaɪnə
bills

Do you have coins for the machine? I only have bills.

(100) Hast du oft Kopfschmerzen? Wenn ja, dann solltest
hast duː ɔft ˈkɔpfʃmɛʁtsən vɛn jaː dan ˈzɔltəst
you have you often headaches if yes then you should

du nicht so lange vor dem Computer sitzen.
duː nɪçt zoː ˈlaŋə foːɐ deːm kɔmˈpjuːtɐ ˈzɪtsn
you not so long in front of the computer to sit

Do you have headaches frequently? If so, then you should not sit at the computer for so long.

(101) Hast du ein Mittel gegen Husten?
hast duː aɪn ˈmɪtl ˈgeːgn ˈhuːstn
you have you a remedy for cough

Do you have medicine for a cough?

(102) Hast du meine neue Adresse?
hast duː ˈmaɪnə ˈnɔɪə aˈdʁɛsə
you have you my new address

Do you have my new address?

(103) Hörst du den Donner? Der Sturm kommt näher.
høːɐst duː deːn ˈdɔnɐ deːɐ ʃtʊʁm kɔmt ˈnɛːɐ
you hear you the thunder the storm it comes closer

Do you hear the thunder? The storm is getting closer.

(104) Kennst du ein gutes Rezept für Gemüsesuppe?
kɛnst duː aɪn ˈguːtəs ʁeˈtsɛpt fyːɐ gəˈmyːzəˌzʊpə
you know you a good recipe for vegetable soup

Do you know a good recipe for vegetable soup?

(105) Kannst du schwimmen?
kanst duː ˈʃvɪmən
you can you to swim

Do you know how to swim?

(106) Kennst du den Unterschied zwischen senkrecht und
kɛnst duː deːn ˈʊntɐʃiːt ˈtsvɪʃn ˈzɛŋkʁɛçt ʊnt
you know you the difference between vertical and

waagerecht?
ˈvaːgəʁɛçt
horizontal

Do you know the difference between vertical and horizontal?

(107) Hättest du etwas dagegen, wenn ich morgen Nachmittag vorbeikomme?
'hɛtəst du: 'ɛtvas da'ge:gn vɛn ɪç 'mɔʁgn 'na:xmɪˌtak fo:ɐ̯'baɪ̯ˌkɔmə
you would have you something against it if I tomorrow afternoon I stop by

Do you mind if I stop by tomorrow afternoon?

(108) Hast du das Haus gekauft oder gemietet?
hast du: da:s haʊs gə'kaʊft 'o:dɐ gə'mi:tət
→→ you the house ←you bought or ←you rented

Do you own your house or do you rent?

(109) Spielst du ein Musikinstrument?
ʃpi:lst du: aɪn mu'zi:kɪnstʁuˌmɛnt
you play you a musical instrument

Do you play a musical instrument?

(110) Versprichst du mir, es niemandem zu verraten?
fɛɐ̯'ʃpʁɪçst du: mi:ɐ̯ ɛs 'ni:mandəm tsu: fɛɐ̯'ʁa:tən
you promise you to me it to nobody to to reveal

Do you promise not to tell anyone?

(111) Rauchst du? – Nein, niemals. Ich trinke auch keinen Alkohol.
ʁaʊxst du: naɪn 'ni:ma:ls ɪç 'tʁɪŋkə aʊx 'kaɪnən 'alkoho:l
you smoke you no never I I drink also no alcohol

Do you smoke? - No, never. I don't drink alcohol either.

(112) Sprechen Sie Englisch? – Ein bisschen.
'ʃpʁɛçn zi: 'ɛŋlɪʃ aɪn 'bɪsçən
you speak you English a little

Do you speak English? - A little.

(113) Trinken Sie Ihren Tee mit Zucker?
'tʁɪŋkn zi: 'i:ʁən te: mɪt 'tsʊkɐ
you drink you your tea with sugar

Do you take sugar in your tea?

(114) Glaubst du, dass du die Stelle bekommen wirst? – Ja, ich sehe das recht optimistisch.
glaʊpst du: das du: di: 'ʃtɛlə bə'kɔmən vɪʁst ja: ɪç 'ze:ə das ʁɛçt ɔpti'mɪstɪʃ
you believe you that you the job you will get yes I I see that quite optimistically

Do you think that you will get the job? - Yes, I am quite optimistic.

(115) Brauchen Sie die Rechnung?
'bʁaʊxn zi: di: 'ʁɛçnʊŋ
you need you the receipt

Do you want a receipt?

(116) Soll ich dich mit nach Hause nehmen?
zɔl ɪç dɪç mɪt na:x 'haʊzə 'ne:mən
I should I you to take home

Do you want a ride home?

(117) Stört es dich, wenn ich rauche?
ʃtø:ɐ̯t ɛs dɪç vɛn ɪç 'ʁaʊxə
it bothers it you if I I smoke

Does it bother you if I smoke?

(118) Habt ihr ein Haustier? – Ja, wir haben einen Hund.
haːpt iːɐ aɪn ˈhaʊsˌtiːɐ jaː viːɐ ˈhaːbn ˈaɪnən hʊnt
you have you a pet yes we we have a dog

Does your family have a pet? - Yes, we have a dog.

(119) Weiß denn nicht jeder, dass Rauchen der Gesundheit
vaɪs dɛn nɪçt ˈjeːdɐ das ˈʁaʊxn deːɐ ɡəˈzʊnthaɪt
he knows ! not everyone that smoking the health

schadet?
ˈʃaːdət
it harms

Doesn't everyone know that smoking is harmful to your health?

(120) Geh mit den nassen Schuhen nicht ins Wohnzimmer.
geː mɪt deːn ˈnasən ˈʃuːən nɪçt ɪns ˈvoːnˌtsɪmɐ
go with the wet shoes not into the living room

Don't go into the living room with wet shoes.

(121) Verrate mir ja nicht das Ende des Films.
fɛɐˈʁaːtə miːɐ jaː nɪçt das ˈɛndə dɛs fɪlms
reveal to me ! not the end of the movie

Don't tell me how the movie ends.

(122) Hast du kein schärferes Messer?
hast duː kaɪn ˈʃɛʁfəʁəs ˈmɛsɐ
you have you no sharper knife

Don't you have a sharper knife?

(123) Willst du deinen Mantel nicht ablegen?
vɪlst duː ˈdaɪnən ˈmantl̩ nɪçt ˈapˌleːɡn̩
you want you your coat not to take off

Don't you want to take off your coat?

(124) Fahr vorsichtig. Die Straßen sind glatt.
faːɐ ˈfoːɐˌzɪçtɪç diː ˈʃtʁaːsən zɪnt ɡlat
drive carefully the streets they are icy

Drive carefully. The roads are icy.

(125) Acht Stunden lang fahren ist zu viel. Stattdessen solltest
axt ˈʃtʊndn̩ laŋ ˈfaːʁən ɪst tsuː fiːl ʃtatˈdɛsn̩ ˈzɔltəst
eight hours long to drive it is too much instead you should

du fliegen.
duː ˈfliːɡn̩
you to fly

Driving eight hours is too much. You should fly instead.

(126) Wegen des Nebels konnte unser Flugzeug nicht landen.
ˈveːɡn̩ dɛs ˈneːbl̩s ˈkɔntə ˈʊnzɐ ˈfluːkˌtsɔɪk nɪçt ˈlandn̩
due to the fog it could our airplane not to land

Due to fog, our plane could not land.

(127) Jedes Land hat seine eigene Kultur.
ˈjeːdəs lant hat ˈzaɪnə ˈaɪɡənə kʊlˈtuːɐ
each country it has its own culture

Each country has its own unique culture.

(128) Acht geteilt durch zwei ist gleich vier.
axt ɡəˈtaɪlt dʊʁç tsvaɪ ɪst ɡlaɪç fiːɐ
eight divided by two equals four

Eight divided by two equals four.

(129) EU-Bürger dürfen überall in Europa arbeiten.
eːˈuːˌbʏʁɡɐ ˈdʏʁfn̩ yːbɐˈal ɪn ɔɪˈʁoːpa ˈaʁbaɪtn̩
EU citizens they are allowed everywhere in Europe to work

EU citizens can work anywhere in Europe.

(130) **Jeder will etwas anderes. Wir müssen einen Kompromiss finden.**
ˈjeːdɐ vɪl ˈɛtvas ˈandəʁəs viːɐ ˈmʏsn̩ ˈaɪnən kɔmpʁoˈmɪs ˈfɪndn̩
everybody he wants something different we we have to a compromise to find

Everybody wants something different. We have to find a compromise.

(131) **Heutzutage reden alle über den Klimawandel.**
ˈhɔɪttsuˌtaːɡə ˈʁeːdn̩ ˈalə ˈyːbɐ deːn ˈkliːmaˌvandl̩
these days they talk everyone about the climate change

Everyone is talking about climate change these days.

(132) **Alle standen auf dem Bahnsteig und winkten zum Abschied.**
ˈalə ˈʃtandn̩ aʊf deːm ˈbaːnʃtaɪk ʊnt ˈvɪŋktən tsʊm ˈapʃiːt
everyone they stood on the platform and they waved goodbye

Everyone stood on the platform and waved goodbye.

(133) **Das kostet insgesamt 2000 Dollar einschließlich der Flüge und Hotels.**
das ˈkɔstət ɪnsɡəˈzamt ˈtsvaɪˌtaʊznt ˈdɔlaʁ ˈaɪnʃliːslɪç deːɐ ˈflyːɡə ʊnt hoˈtɛls
that it costs in total two thousand dollars including the flights and hotels

Everything together costs 2000 dollars including flights and hotels.

(134) **Entschuldige die Störung, aber es gibt ein Problem.**
ɛntˈʃʊldɪɡə diː ˈʃtøːʁʊŋ ˈaːbɐ ɛs ɡiːpt aɪn pʁoˈbleːm
pardon the disturbance but there is a problem

Excuse me for disturbing you, but there is a problem.

(135) **Die Familie ist das Wichtigste im Leben.**
diː faˈmiːliə ɪst daːs ˈvɪçtɪçstə ɪm ˈleːbn̩
the family it is the most important in the life

Family is the most important thing.

(136) **Das Füttern der Tiere im Zoo ist verboten.**
das ˈfʏtɐn deːɐ ˈtiːʁə ɪm tsoː ɪst fɛɐˈboːtn̩
the feeding of the animals at the zoo it is forbidden

Feeding the animals at the zoo is forbidden.

(137) **Mach vor dem Fernsehen deine Hausaufgaben fertig.**
max foːɐ deːm ˈfɛʁnˌzeːən ˈdaɪnə ˈhaʊsaʊfˌɡaːbn̩ ˈfɛʁtɪç
complete→ before the watching TV your homework ←

Finish your homework before watching television.

(138) **Markiere zuerst die Zeilen, dann kopiere sie und füge sie ins neue Dokument ein.**
maʁˈkiːʁə tsuˈeːɐst diː ˈtsaɪlən dan koˈpiːʁə ziː ʊnt ˈfyːɡə ziː ɪns ˈnɔɪə dokuˈmɛnt aɪn
highlight first the lines then copy them and paste→ them into the new document ←

First highlight the lines, then copy and paste into a new document.

(139) **Schnall dich zuerst an und dann fahr los.**
ʃnal dɪç tsuˈeːɐst an ʊnt dan faːɐ loːs
buckle up→ first ← and then drive off

First put on your seatbelt and then start driving.

(140) **Zieh zuerst deine Socken an und danach die Schuhe.**
tsi: tsuˈeːɐst ˈdaɪnə ˈzɔkn̩ an ʊnt daˈnaːx diː ˈʃuːə
put on→ first your socks ← and then the shoes

First put on your socks and then put on your shoes.

(141) **Zuerst gehen wir Lebensmittel einkaufen und dann grillen wir im Garten.**
tsuˈeːɐst ˈgeːən viːɐ ˈleːbnsˌmɪtl̩ ˈaɪnˌkaʊfn̩ ʊnt dan ˈgʁɪlən viːɐ ɪm ˈgaʁtn̩
first we go we groceries to shop and then we grill we in the yard

First we're going food shopping, then we're barbecuing in the yard.

(142) **Bei »Familienstand« musst du »ledig« ankreuzen, da du ja nicht verheiratet bist.**
baɪ faˈmiːliənʃtant mʊst duː ˈleːdɪç ˈanˌkʁɔɪtsn̩ daː duː jaː nɪçt fɛɐˈhaɪʁaːtət bɪst
for marital status you have you single to mark because you ! not married you are

For "marital status" you have to mark "single" since you're not married.

(143) **Zum Nachtisch gibt es Schokoladeneis.**
tsʊm ˈnaːxˌtɪʃ giːpt ɛs ʃokoˈlaːdn̩ˌaɪs
for the dessert there is chocolate ice cream

For dessert there is chocolate ice cream.

(144) **Zu Mittag gibt es Hühnchen mit Reis.**
tsuː ˈmɪtaːk giːpt ɛs ˈhyːnçən mɪt ʁaɪs
for lunch there is chicken with rice

For lunch there is chicken with rice.

(145) **Mir ist nicht nur der Preis wichtig, sondern auch die Qualität.**
miːɐ ɪst nɪçt nuːɐ deːɐ pʁaɪs ˈvɪçtɪç ˈzɔndɐn aʊx diː kvaliˈtɛːt
for me it is not only→ the price important ←but also the quality

For me, not only is the price important, but also the quality.

(146) **Bei dieser Aufgabe stehen drei Themen zur Auswahl.**
baɪ ˈdiːzɐ ˈaʊfˌgaːbə ˈʃteːən dʁaɪ ˈteːmən tsuːɐ ˈaʊsvaːl
for this assignment they are available→ three topics ←

For the assignment you can choose from these three topics.

(147) **Zum letzten Mal, die Antwort lautet Nein.**
tsʊm ˈlɛtstən maːl diː ˈantvɔʁt ˈlaʊtət naɪn
for the last time the answer it is no

For the last time, the answer is no.

(148) **Von jetzt an gehe ich regelmäßig ins Fitnessstudio.**
fɔn jɛtst an ˈgeːə ɪç ˈʁeːglˌmɛːsɪç ɪns ˈfɪtnɛsˌʃtuːdio
from now on I go I regularly to the gym

From now on I will go to the gym regularly.

(149) **Die Müllabfuhr kommt zweimal die Woche.**
diː ˈmʏlˌapfuːɐ kɔmt ˈtsvaɪmaːl diː ˈvɔxə
the garbage collection it comes twice per week

Garbage collection comes twice a week.

(150) Die Benzinpreise sind in letzter Zeit viel höher als sonst.
diː bɛnˈtsiːnˌpʁaɪzə zɪnt ɪn ˈlɛtstɐ tsaɪt fiːl ˈhøːɐ als zɔnst
the gas prices they are lately much higher than usual

Gasoline prices are much higher than normal lately.

(151) Lass mich eine Minute darüber nachdenken.
las mɪç ˈaɪnə miˈnuːtə daˈʁyːbɐ ˈnaːxˌdɛŋkn̩
let me a minute about it to think

Give me a minute to think about it.

(152) Erzähle mir jede Einzelheit über dein Date.
ɛɐˈtsɛːlə miːɐ ˈjeːdə ˈaɪntslhaɪt ˈyːbɐ daɪn deɪt
tell me every detail about your date

Give me all the details about your date.

(153) Eine grüne Hose mit gelben Schuhen? Das sieht
ˈaɪnə ˈɡʁyːnə ˈhoːzə mɪt ˈɡɛlbən ˈʃuːən das ziːt
a green pair of pants with yellow shoes that it looks →

komisch aus.
ˈkoːmɪʃ aʊs
funny ←

Green pants and yellow shoes? That looks funny.

(154) Alles Gute zum Geburtstag!
ˈaləs ˈɡuːtə tsʊm ɡəˈbuːɐtsˌtaːk
all the best to the birthday

Happy birthday!

(155) Schönes Wochenende. – Danke, dir auch.
ˈʃøːnəs ˈvɔxnˌɛndə ˈdaŋkə diːɐ aʊx
nice weekend thanks to you too

Have a nice weekend. - Thanks, you too.

(156) Hast du dir schon die Zähne geputzt?
hast duː diːɐ ʃoːn diː ˈtsɛːnə ɡəˈpʊtst
→ already the teeth ← you have cleaned

Have you already brushed your teeth?

(157) Hast du schon deine Hausaufgaben für die Schule
hast duː ʃoːn ˈdaɪnə ˈhaʊsaʊfˌɡaːbn̩ fyːɐ diː ˈʃuːlə
→ you already your homework for the school

gemacht?
ɡəˈmaːxt
← you have done

Have you already done your homework for school?

(158) Hast du schon was gegessen?
hast duː ʃoːn vas ɡəˈɡɛsn̩
→ you already something ← you have eaten

Have you already eaten?

(159) Weißt du schon, was du bestellen möchtest?
vaɪst duː ʃoːn vas duː bəˈʃtɛlən ˈmϾçtəst
you know you already what you you would like to order

Have you decided what you would like to order?

(160) Warst du schon mal an der Ostsee?
vaʁst duː ʃoːn maːl an deːɐ ˈɔstˌzeː
you were you ever at the Baltic Sea

Have you ever been to the Baltic Sea?

(161) Hast du zufällig meine Brille gesehen?
hast duː ˈtsuːfɛlɪç ˈmaɪnə ˈbʁɪlə ɡəˈzeːən
→ you by any chance my glasses ← you have seen

Have you, by any chance, seen my glasses?

(162) Er hat meine Hausaufgaben abgeschrieben, trotzdem hat
 eːɐ hat ˈmaɪnə ˈhaʊsaʊfˌgaːbn ˈapgəʃʁiːbn ˈtʁɔtsdeːm hat
 he → my homework ←he copied nevertheless →
 er irgendwie eine bessere Note als ich bekommen.
 eːɐ ˈɪʁgntˈviː ˈaɪnə ˈbɛsəʁə ˈnoːtə als ɪç bəˈkɔmən
 he somehow a better grade then me ←he got

He copied my homework but somehow got a better grade than me.

(163) Er hat viele Geschenke zum Geburtstag bekommen.
 eːɐ hat ˈfiːlə gəˈʃɛŋkə tsʊm gəˈbuːɐtsˌtaːk bəˈkɔmən
 he → many gifts for the birthday ←he got

He got many gifts for his birthday.

(164) Er ist erkältet und kann nicht durch die Nase atmen.
 eːɐ ɪst ɛɐˈkɛltət ʊnt kan nɪçt dʊʁç diː ˈnaːzə ˈaːtmən
 he he has a cold and he can not through the nose to breathe

He has a cold and can not breathe through his nose.

(165) Er ist von Geburt an blind.
 eːɐ ɪst fɔn gəˈbuːɐt an blɪnt
 he he is from birth blind

He has been blind from birth.

(166) Er liegt seit drei Wochen im Koma.
 eːɐ liːkt zaɪt dʁaɪ ˈvɔxən ɪm ˈkoːma
 he he lies for three weeks in the coma

He has been in a coma for three weeks.

(167) Er hat sich verletzt und musste in die Notaufnahme.
 eːɐ hat zɪç fɛɐˈlɛtst ʊnt ˈmʊstə ɪn diː ˈnoːtaʊfˌnaːmə
 he he hurt himself and he had to in the emergency room

He hurt himself and had to go to the emergency room.

(168) Er ist Schauspieler und zudem ein großartiger Sänger.
 eːɐ ɪst ˈʃaʊʃpiːlɐ ʊnt tsuˈdeːm aɪn ˈgʁoːsˌaːɐtɪgɐ ˈzɛŋɐ
 he he is actor and in addition a great singer

He is an actor and also a great singer.

(169) Er ist ein durchschnittlicher Schüler, aber ein
 eːɐ ɪst aɪn ˈdʊʁçʃnɪtlɪçɐ ˈʃyːlɐ ˈaːbɐ aɪn
 he he is an average student but an
 hervorragender Sportler.
 hɛɐˈfoːɐˌʁaːgndɐ ˈʃpɔʁtlɐ
 excellent athlete

He is an average student but an excellent athlete.

(170) Er sieht genauso aus wie sein Vater.
 eːɐ ziːt gəˈnaʊzoː aʊs viː zaɪn ˈfaːtɐ
 he he looks→ just ← like his father

He looks just like his father.

(171) Für einen Anfänger ist er ziemlich gut im Tennis.
 fyːɐ ˈaɪnən ˈanfɛŋɐ ɪst eːɐ ˈtsiːmlɪç guːt ɪm ˈtɛnɪs
 for a beginner he is he pretty good in the tennis

He plays tennis quite well for a beginner.

(172) Er lief einen Marathon und rannte als Erster durchs
 eːɐ liːf ˈaɪnən ˈmaːʁatɔn ʊnt ˈʁantə als ˈeːɐstɐ dʊʁçs
 he he ran a marathon and he ran first through the
 Ziel.
 tsiːl
 finish

He ran a marathon and finished in first place.

(173) Er hat wirklich einen Urlaub verdient.
eːɐ hat ˈvɪʁklɪç ˈaɪnən ˈuːɐlaʊp fɛɐˈdiːnt
he → really a vacation ←he deserved

He really deserves a vacation.

(174) Er hat mein Hilfsangebot abgelehnt.
eːɐ hat maɪn ˈhɪlfsangəˌboːt ˈapgəˌleːnt
he → my offer of help ←he refused

He refused my offer of help.

(175) Er leidet an einer ernsten Krankheit.
eːɐ ˈlaɪdət an ˈaɪnɐ ˈɛʁnstən ˈkʁaŋkhaɪt
he he suffers from a serious illness

He suffers from a serious illness.

(176) Er hält sich für schlauer, als er in Wahrheit ist.
eːɐ hɛlt zɪç fyːɐ ˈʃlaʊɐ als eːɐ ɪn ˈvaːɐhaɪt ɪst
he he thinks of himself as smarter than he in truth he is

He thinks he is smarter than he really is.

(177) Er sagte, dass er zur Party komme, aber verspätet sei.
eːɐ ˈzaːktə das eːɐ tsuːɐ ˈpaʁti ˈkɔmə ˈaːbɐ fɛɐˈʃpɛːtət zaɪ
he he said that he to the party he comes but late he is

He told me that he is coming to the party but will be late.

(178) Er hat sich viel Mühe gegeben, etwas Leckeres zu
eːɐ hat zɪç fiːl ˈmyːə gəˈgeːbn ˈɛtvas ˈlɛkɐɐs tsuː
he → much ←he took the trouble something tasty to

kochen.
ˈkɔxn
to cook

He tried very hard to cook something tasty.

(179) Er nimmt den Job nur an, wenn die Firma für seine
eːɐ nɪmt deːn dʒɔp nuːɐ an vɛn diː ˈfɪʁma fyːɐ ˈzaɪnə
he he accepts→ the job only ← if the company for his

Umzugskosten aufkommt.
ˈʊmˌtsuːksˈkɔstn ˈaʊfˌkɔmt
moving expenses it pays

He will only accept the job if the company pays for his moving expenses.

(180) Er arbeitet in der medizinischen Forschung.
eːɐ ˈaʁbaɪtət ɪn deːɐ mediˈtsiːnɪʃn ˈfɔʁʃʊŋ
he he works in the medical research

He works in medical research.

(181) Er kann unter Druck gut arbeiten.
eːɐ kan ˈʊntɐ dʁʊk guːt ˈaʁbaɪtn
he he can under pressure well to work

He works well under pressure.

(182) Hallo, wie geht es dir? - Gut, danke, und dir?
haˈloː viː geːt ɛs diːɐ guːt ˈdaŋkə ʊnt diːɐ
hello how it goes it for you good thank and for you

Hello, how are you? - Good, thanks, and you?

(183) Hier sind meine Wohnungsschlüssel. Kannst du meine
hiːɐ zɪnt ˈmaɪnə ˈvoːnʊŋsˌʃlʏsl kanst duː ˈmaɪnə
here they are my apartment keys you can you my

Blumen gießen, während ich weg bin?
ˈbluːmən ˈgiːsn ˈvɛːʁənt ɪç vɛk bɪn
flowers to water while I away I am

Here are the keys to my apartment. Can you water my flowers while I'm gone?

(184) Hier ist meine Büronummer und auch meine Handynummer.
hiːɐ ɪst ˈmaɪnə byˈʁoːˌnʊmɐ ʊnt aʊx ˈmaɪnə ˈhɛndiˌnʊmɐ
here it is my office number and also my cell phone number

Here is my office number and also my cell phone number.

(185) Das ist das Buch, von dem ich dir erzählt habe.
das ɪst daːs buːx fɔn deːm ɪç diːɐ ɛɐˈtsɛːlt ˈhaːbə
this it is the book of which I to you I told

Here is the book I was telling you about.

(186) Hier ist die Zutatenliste für den Kuchen.
hiːɐ ɪst diː ˈtsuːtaːtn̩ˌlɪstə fyːɐ deːn ˈkuːxn̩
here it is the ingredients list for the cake

Here is the list of ingredients needed for the cake.

(187) Er tut so, als hätten wir nie darüber gesprochen.
eːɐ tuːt zoː als ˈhɛtən viːɐ niː daˈʁyːbɐ gəˈʃpʁɔxn̩
he he acts as though → we never about it ←we have spoken

He's acting as though we never spoke about that.

(188) Die Kündigung der Firma traf ihn überraschend.
diː ˈkʏndɪgʊŋ deːɐ ˈfɪʁma tʁaːf iːn yːbɐˈʁaʃnt
the dismissal from the company it struck him by surprise

His dismissal from the company came as a surprise.

(189) Gib mir deine Hand. Wir gehen über die Straße.
giːp miːɐ ˈdaɪnə hant viːɐ ˈgeːən yːbɐ diː ˈʃtʁaːsə
give to me your hand we we go across the street

Hold my hand. We're crossing the street.

(190) Wohnen wird immer teurer.
ˈvoːnən vɪʁt ˈɪmɐ ˈtɔɪʁɐ
housing it becomes always more expensive

Housing is becoming more and more expensive.

(191) Wie entsorgt man alte Handys?
viː ɛntˈzɔʁkt man ˈaltə ˈhɛndis
how one disposes of one old cell phones

How can I dispose of my old cell phone?

(192) Wie ist dir das denn eingefallen?
viː ɪst diːɐ daːs dɛn ˈaɪngəˌfalən
how → that ! ←you came up with

How did you come up with this idea?

(193) Wie habt ihr euch kennengelernt?
viː haːpt iːɐ ɔɪç ˈkɛnəngəˌlɛʁnt
how → you each other ←you met

How did you two meet?

(194) Wie spielt man dieses Spiel? Kennst du die Regeln?
viː ʃpiːlt man ˈdiːzəs ʃpiːl kɛnst duː diː ˈʁeːgln̩
how one plays one this game you know you the rules

How do you play this game? Do you know the rules?

(195) Wie schreibt man dieses Wort?
viː ˈʃʁaɪpt man ˈdiːzəs vɔʁt
how one writes one that word

How do you spell that word?

(196) **Wie weit ist es bis zu deinem Freund? – Nicht weit, nur zehn Minuten von hier.**
viː vaɪt ɪst ɛs bɪs tsuː ˈdaɪnəm ˈfʁɔɪnt nɪçt vaɪt nuːɐ tseːn miˈnuːtən fɔn hiːɐ
how far it is it to your friend not far only ten minutes from here

How far is it to your friend's house? - It is very close, only ten minutes from here.

(197) **Wie viele Zigaretten rauchen Sie am Tag? Alles über null ist zu viel.**
viː ˈfiːlə tsigaˈʁɛtn̩ ˈʁaʊxn̩ ziː am taːk ˈaləs ˈyːbɐ nʊl ɪst tsuː fiːl
how many cigarettes you smoke you per day anything above zero it is too many

How many cigarettes do you smoke a day? Anything more than zero is too many.

(198) **Wie viele Länder haben Sie schon bereist?**
viː ˈfiːlə ˈlɛndɐ ˈhaːbn̩ ziː ʃoːn bəˈʁaɪst
how many countries → you already ←you have traveled to

How many countries have you visited?

(199) **Wie viele Buchstaben gibt es im Alphabet Ihrer Sprache?**
viː ˈfiːlə ˈbuːxʃtaːbn̩ giːpt ɛs ɪm alfaˈbeːt ˈiːʁɐ ˈʃpʁaːxə
how many letters there are in the alphabet of your language

How many letters does the alphabet have in your language?

(200) **Wie viel Geld schulde ich dir?**
viː fiːl gɛlt ˈʃʊldə ɪç diːɐ
how much money I owe I to you

How much money do I owe you?

(201) **Wie alt ist der Chef? – Keine Ahnung, um die Fünfzig vielleicht.**
viː alt ɪst deːɐ ʃɛf ˈkaɪnə ˈaːnʊŋ ʊm diː ˈfʏnftsɪç fiˈlaɪçt
how old he is the boss no idea around the fifty perhaps

How old is the boss? - I don't know, I guess around fifty.

(202) **Ich habe schon zweimal angerufen, aber keiner hat abgehoben.**
ɪç ˈhaːbə ʃoːn ˈtsvaɪmaːl ˈangəˌʁuːfn̩ ˈaːbɐ ˈkaɪnɐ hat ˈapgəˌhoːbn̩
I → already twice ←I called but nobody he picked up

I already called twice, but nobody answered.

(203) **Ich kenne schon einige Leute in dieser Stadt.**
ɪç ˈkɛnə ʃoːn ˈaɪnɪgə ˈlɔɪtə ɪn ˈdiːzɐ ʃtat
I I know already several people in this city

I already know several people in this city.

(204) **Ich kaufe mein Brot beim Bäcker, und nicht im Supermarkt.**
ɪç ˈkaʊfə maɪn bʁoːt baɪm ˈbɛkɐ ʊnt nɪçt ɪm ˈzuːpɐˌmaʁkt
I I buy my bread at the baker and not in the supermarket

I always buy bread from the baker, not in the supermarket.

(205) Ich muss meinen Kindern abends immer eine Geschichte vorlesen.
ɪç mʊs ˈmaɪnən ˈkɪndɐn ˈaːbnts ˈɪmɐ ˈaɪnə ɡəˈʃɪçtə ˈfoːɐ̯ˌleːzn̩
I I have to my children in the evenings always a story to read (aloud)

I always have to read my children a story in the evening.

(206) In der Stadt fahre ich immer mit den öffentlichen Verkehrsmitteln.
ɪn deːɐ̯ ʃtat ˈfaːʁə ɪç ˈɪmɐ mɪt deːn ˈœfntlɪçən fɛɐ̯ˈkeːɐ̯sˌmɪtl̩n
in the city I drive I always with the public means of transport

I always take public transportation in the city.

(207) Nach 10 Kilometern Laufen bin ich immer erschöpft.
naːx tseːn kiloˈmeːtɐn ˈlaʊfn̩ bɪn ɪç ˈɪmɐ ɛɐ̯ˈʃœpft
after ten kilometers of running I am I always exhausted

I am always exhausted after running 10 km.

(208) Ich bin bei Prüfungen immer sehr nervös.
ɪç bɪn baɪ ˈpʁyːfʊŋən ˈɪmɐ zeːɐ̯ nɛɐ̯ˈvøːs
I I am during tests always very nervous

I am always very nervous during exams.

(209) Ich bin mit der Lage der Wohnung zufrieden.
ɪç bɪn mɪt deːɐ̯ ˈlaːɡə deːɐ̯ ˈvoːnʊŋ tsuˈfʁiːdn̩
I I am with the location of the apartment happy

I am happy with the location of the apartment.

(210) Ich muss mich beeilen. Ich bin spät dran.
ɪç mʊs mɪç bəˈaɪlən ɪç bɪn ʃpɛːt dʁan
I I have to to hurry I I am late

I am in a hurry. I'm late.

(211) Ich interessiere mich für andere Länder und Kulturen.
ɪç ɪntəʁɛˈsiːʁə mɪç fyːɐ̯ ˈandəʁə ˈlɛndɐ ʊnt kʊlˈtuːʁən
I I am interested in other countries and cultures

I am interested in other countries and cultures.

(212) Zum Glück wohnen meine Enkel alle in der Nähe.
tsʊm ɡlʏk ˈvoːnən ˈmaɪnə ˈɛŋkl̩ ˈalə ɪn deːɐ̯ ˈnɛːə
fortunately they live my grandchildren all nearby

I am lucky that all my grandchildren live nearby.

(213) Ich bin neu im Haus. Ich kenne noch keine Nachbarn.
ɪç bɪn nɔɪ ɪm haʊs ɪç ˈkɛnə nɔx ˈkaɪnə ˈnaxbaːɐ̯n
I I am new in the building I I know yet no neighbors

I am new to the building. I don't know any neighbors yet.

(214) Ich habe im Moment keinen Hunger. Ich will nichts essen.
ɪç ˈhaːbə ɪm moˈmɛnt ˈkaɪnən ˈhʊŋɐ ɪç vɪl nɪçts ˈɛsn̩
I I have right now no hunger I I want nothing to eat

I am not hungry right now. I don't want to eat anything.

(215) Ich interessiere mich nicht für Politik.
ɪç ɪntəʁɛˈsiːʁə mɪç nɪçt fyːɐ̯ poliˈtiːk
I I am not interested in politics

I am not interested in politics.

(216) Ich bin stolz auf dich. Das hast du toll gemacht.
ɪç bɪn ʃtɔlts aʊf dɪç das hast duː tɔl ɡəˈmaːxt
I I am proud of you that → you great ←you did

I am proud of you. You did a great job.

(217) **Es überrascht mich, dass die Wohnung so günstig ist. Ich**
ɛs yːbɐˈʁaʃt mɪç das diː ˈvoːnʊŋ zoː ˈɡʏnstɪç ɪst ɪç
it it surprises me that the apartment so low-priced it is I

frage mich, was damit nicht stimmt.
ˈfʁaːɡə mɪç vas daˈmɪt nɪçt ʃtɪmt
I wonder what with it not it is right

I am quite surprised that the apartment is so cheap. I wonder what's wrong with it.

(218) **Ich bin der Jüngste in der Familie.**
ɪç bɪn deːɐ ˈjʏŋstə ɪn deːɐ faˈmiːliə
I I am the youngest one in the family

I am the youngest in our family.

(219) **Ich habe mir eine Digitaluhr gekauft. Sie ist viel**
ɪç ˈhaːbə miːɐ ˈaɪnə diɡiˈtaːlˌuːɐ ɡəˈkaʊft ziː ɪst fiːl
I → myself a digital watch ←I bought it it is much

genauer als meine alte Mechanikuhr.
ɡəˈnaʊɐ als ˈmaɪnə ˈaltə meˈçaːnɪkˌuːɐ
more accurate than my old mechanical watch

I bought a digital watch. It runs more accurately than my old wind-up watch.

(220) **Ich habe mir kein neues, sondern ein gebrauchtes Auto**
ɪç ˈhaːbə miːɐ kaɪn ˈnɔɪəs ˈzɔndɐn aɪn ɡəˈbʁaʊxtəs ˈaʊto
I → myself not a new but rather a used car

gekauft.
ɡəˈkaʊft
←I bought

I bought a used car, not a new one.

(221) **Ich habe mehr Orangen gekauft, als ich brauche.**
ɪç ˈhaːbə meːɐ oˈʁãːʒn ɡəˈkaʊft als ɪç ˈbʁaʊxə
I → more oranges ←I bought than I I need

I bought more oranges than I know what to do with.

(222) **Ich habe mir einen größeren Computerbildschirm gekauft.**
ɪç ˈhaːbə miːɐ ˈaɪnən ˈɡʁøːsɐɐn kɔmˈpjuːtɐˌbɪltʃɪʁm ɡəˈkaʊft
I → myself a bigger computer screen ←I bought

Er ist besser für die Augen.
eːɐ ɪst ˈbɛsɐ fyːɐ diː ˈaʊɡən
it it is better for the eyes

I bought myself a bigger computer monitor. It's better for my eyes.

(223) **Ich habe mir einen dunkelblauen Anzug gekauft.**
ɪç ˈhaːbə miːɐ ˈaɪnən ˈdʊŋkəlˌblaʊən ˈanˌtsuːk ɡəˈkaʊft
I → myself a dark blue suit ←I bought

I bought myself a dark blue suit.

(224) **Diese Sonnenbrille habe ich in Europa gekauft.**
ˈdiːzə ˈzɔnənˌbʁɪlə ˈhaːbə ɪç ɪn ɔɪˈʁoːpa ɡəˈkaʊft
these sunglasses → I in Europe ←I bought

I bought these sunglasses in Europe.

(225) **Ich kann mich kaum bewegen, ohne Schmerzen zu haben.**
ɪç kan mɪç kaʊm bəˈveːɡn̩ ˈoːnə ˈʃmɛʁtsn̩ tsuː ˈhaːbn̩
I I can → barely ←to move without pains to to have

I can barely move without pain.

(226) Das kann ich nicht selber entscheiden, weil ich erst den
das kan ɪç nɪçt ˈzɛlbɐ ɛntˈʃaɪdn vaɪl ɪç eːɐst deːn
that I can I not myself to decide because I first the
Chef fragen muss.
ʃɛf ˈfʁaːgn mʊs
boss to ask I have to

I can not decide that myself because I have to ask the boss first.

(227) Ich spreche sehr gutes Englisch, Französisch und Persisch.
ɪç ˈʃpʁɛçə zeːɐ ˈguːtəs ˈɛŋlɪʃ fʁanˈtsøːzɪʃ ʊnt ˈpɛʁzɪʃ
I I speak very good English French and Persian

I can speak English, French, and Persian very well.

(228) Ich kann gerade nicht ans Telefon gehen, also hinterlasse
ɪç kan gəˈʁaːdə nɪçt ans ˈteːləfoːn ˈgeːən ˈalzo hɪntɐˈlasə
I I can right now not to answer the telephone so leave
bitte eine Nachricht.
ˈbɪtə ˈaɪnə ˈnaːxʁɪçt
please a message

I can't answer my phone right now, so please leave a message.

(229) Ich bekomme keinen Bissen mehr runter. Ich platze!
ɪç bəˈkɔmə ˈkaɪnən ˈbɪsn meːɐ ˈʁʊntɐ ɪç ˈplatsə
I I get not a bite more down I I am bursting

I can't eat any more. I'm stuffed!

(230) Ich kann mir nicht erklären, wie die Schokolade
ɪç kan miːɐ nɪçt ɛɐˈklɛːʁən viː diː ʃokoˈlaːdə
I I can myself not to explain how the chocolate
verschwunden ist.
fɛɐˈʃvʊndn ɪst
it disappeared

I can't explain how the chocolate disappeared.

(231) Ich kann meine Schlüssel nirgends finden.
ɪç kan ˈmaɪnə ˈʃlʏsl ˈnɪʁgnts ˈfɪndn
I I can my keys nowhere to find

I can't find my keys anywhere.

(232) Mein Gehör ist nicht mehr so gut.
maɪn gəˈhøːɐ ɪst nɪçt meːɐ zoː guːt
my hearing it is no longer so good

I can't hear so well anymore.

(233) Ich kann dir gerade nicht helfen. Ich bin mitten beim
ɪç kan diːɐ gəˈʁaːdə nɪçt ˈhɛlfn ɪç bɪn ˈmɪtn baɪm
I I can you right now not to help I I am in the middle of the
Kochen.
ˈkɔxn
cooking

I can't help you right now. I'm in the middle of cooking dinner.

(234) Ich kann deine Handschrift nicht lesen.
ɪç kan ˈdaɪnə ˈhantʃʁɪft nɪçt ˈleːzn
I I can your handwriting not to read

I can't read your handwriting.

(235) Ich kann nicht laufen, weil mir ein Zeh wehtut.
ɪç kan nɪçt ˈlaʊfn vaɪl miːɐ aɪn tseː ˈveːtuːt
I I can not to run because to me a toe it hurts

I can't run because of pain in one of my toes.

(236) Ich kann nichts verstehen, wenn ihr alle gleichzeitig redet.
ɪç kan nɪçts fɛɐ̯ˈʃteːən vɛn iːɐ̯ ˈalə ˈɡlaɪçˌtsaɪtɪç ˈʁeːdət
I I can nothing to understand when you all at once you speak

I can't understand anything when you all speak at the same time.

(237) Ich kann's nicht erwarten, dich wiederzusehen.
ɪç kans nɪçt ɛɐ̯ˈvaʁtn̩ dɪç ˈviːdɐtsuˌzeːən
I I can (it) not to wait you to see again

I can't wait to see you again.

(238) Ich erkälte mich jeden Winter mindestens einmal.
ɪç ɛɐ̯ˈkɛltə mɪç ˈjeːdn̩ ˈvɪntɐ ˈmɪndəstn̩s ˈaɪnmaːl
I I catch a cold every winter at least once

I catch a cold at least once every winter.

(239) Nachdem ich die Neuigkeiten erfahren hatte, änderte ich
naːxˈdeːm ɪç diː ˈnɔɪçkaɪtən ɛɐ̯ˈfaːʁən ˈhatə ˈɛndɐtə ɪç
after I the new information I had learned I changed I

meine Meinung.
ˈmaɪnə ˈmaɪnʊŋ
my opinion

I changed my opinion after getting new information.

(240) Ich habe die Rechnung überprüft. Alles ist in Ordnung.
ɪç ˈhaːbə diː ˈʁɛçnʊŋ yːbɐˈpʁyːft ˈaləs ɪst ɪn ˈɔʁdnʊŋ
I → the bill ←I checked everything it is okay

I checked the bill. Everything is correct.

(241) Den Termin habe ich völlig vergessen.
deːn tɛɐ̯ˈmiːn ˈhaːbə ɪç ˈfœlɪç fɛɐ̯ˈɡɛsn̩
the appointment → I completely ←I forgot

I completely forgot about the appointment.

(242) Ich habe dir etwas Besonderes gekocht.
ɪç ˈhaːbə diːɐ̯ ˈɛtvas bəˈzɔndəʁəs ɡəˈkɔxt
I → for you something special ←I cooked

I cooked a special meal for you.

(243) Durch den ganzen Dreck am Fenster konnte ich nichts
dʊʁç deːn ˈɡantsən dʁɛk am ˈfɛnstɐ ˈkɔntə ɪç nɪçts
through the entire dirt on the window I could I nothing

sehen.
ˈzeːən
to see

I couldn't see anything because of all the dirt on the window.

(244) Ich musste nichts zahlen. Die Reparatur wurde von der
ɪç ˈmʊstə nɪçts ˈtsaːlən diː ʁepaʁaˈtuːɐ̯ ˈvʊʁdə fɔn deːɐ̯
I I had to nothing to pay the repair → by the

Garantie abgedeckt.
ɡaʁanˈtiː ˈapɡəˌdɛkt
warranty ←it was covered

I did not have to pay anything. The repair was covered by the warranty.

(245) Mir war gar nicht klar, dass es schon so spät ist. Ich
miːɐ̯ vaːɐ̯ ɡaːɐ̯ nɪçt klaːɐ̯ das ɛs ʃoːn zoː ʃpɛːt ɪst ɪç
to me it was not at all clear that it already so late it was I

muss los.
mʊs loːs
I have to go

I did not realize it was already so late. I have to go.

(246) **Ich habe deine Frage nicht verstanden. Kannst du sie bitte wiederholen?**
ɪç 'ha:bə 'daɪnə 'fʁa:gə nɪçt fɛɐ̯'ʃtandn̩ kanst du: zi: 'bɪtə vi:dɐ'ho:lən
I → your question not ←I understood you can you it please to repeat

I didn't understand your question. Please repeat it.

(247) **Ich weiß nicht, ob wir diesen Schuh in Ihrer Größe haben. Ich schaue mal im Lager nach.**
ɪç vaɪs nɪçt ɔp vi:ɐ̯ 'di:zən ʃu: ɪn 'i:ʁɐ 'gʁø:sə 'ha:bn̩ ɪç 'ʃaʊə ma:l ɪm 'la:gɐ na:x
I I know not if we this shoe in your size we have I I check→ ! in the stock room ←

I do not know if we have this shoe in your size. I'll check the stock room.

(248) **Ich bade nicht gern, ich dusche lieber.**
ɪç 'ba:də nɪçt gɛɐ̯n ɪç 'du:ʃə 'li:bɐ
I I bathe not gladly I I shower preferably

I don't like baths, I prefer showers.

(249) **Meine Kinder dürfen nicht länger als dreißig Minuten pro Tag fernsehen.**
'maɪnə 'kɪndɐ 'dyʁfn̩ nɪçt 'lɛŋɐ als 'dʁaɪsɪç mi'nu:tən pʁo: ta:k 'fɛɐ̯n,ze:ən
my kids they are allowed not longer than thirty minutes per day to watch TV

I don't allow my kids to watch TV for more than thirty minutes per day.

(250) **Ich bezweifle ja nicht, dass du Recht hast, aber du musst immer noch alle anderen überzeugen.**
ɪç bə'tsvaɪflə ja: nɪçt das du: ʁɛçt hast 'a:bɐ du: mʊst 'ɪmɐ nɔx 'alə 'andəʁən y:bɐ'tsɔɪgn̩
I I doubt ! not that you you are right but you you have to still all the others to convince

I don't doubt that you're right, but you still have to convince everyone else.

(251) **Ich verdiene nicht genug Geld, um mir ein neues Auto leisten zu können.**
ɪç fɛɐ̯'di:nə nɪçt gə'nu:k gɛlt ʊm mi:ɐ̯ aɪn 'nɔɪəs 'aʊto 'laɪstn̩ tsu: 'kœnən
I I earn not enough money to for me a new car to afford to to be able

I don't earn enough money to afford a new car.

(252) **Mir geht's nicht gut. Ich glaube, ich habe Fieber.**
mi:ɐ̯ ge:ts nɪçt gu:t ɪç 'glaʊbə ɪç 'ha:bə 'fi:bɐ
for me it goes not well I I think I I have fever

I don't feel well. I think I have a fever.

(253) **Ich habe zwar kein Festnetz, aber dafür ein Handy.**
ɪç 'ha:bə tsva:ɐ̯ kaɪn 'fɛst,nɛts 'a:bɐ da'fy:ɐ̯ aɪn 'hɛndi
I I have indeed no landline but instead a cell phone

I don't have a landline, but I have a cell phone.

(254) Ich habe noch keine eigene Wohnung. Ich wohne vorläufig bei einem Freund.
ɪç 'ha:bə nɔx 'kaɪnə 'aɪgənə 'vo:nʊŋ ɪç 'vo:nə 'fo:ɐlɔɪfɪç baɪ 'aɪnəm 'fʁɔɪnt
I I have yet no own apartment I I live for the time being with a friend

I don't have an apartment yet. I'm living with a friend for the time being.

(255) Ich habe noch keine Kinder, aber ich hoffe, dass ich irgendwann einmal drei habe.
ɪç 'ha:bə nɔx 'kaɪnə 'kɪndɐ 'a:bɐ ɪç 'hɔfə das ɪç 'ɪʁgənt'van 'aɪnma:l dʁaɪ 'ha:bə
I I have yet no kids but I I hope that I eventually three I have

I don't have kids yet, but I hope to eventually have three.

(256) Dieses Wort kenne ich nicht. Ich sollte es mal im Wörterbuch nachschlagen.
'di:zəs vɔʁt 'kɛnə ɪç nɪçt ɪç 'zɔltə ɛs ma:l ɪm 'vœʁtɐˌbu:x 'na:xˌʃla:gn̩
that word I know I not I I should it ! in the dictionary to look up

I don't know that word. I should look it up in the dictionary.

(257) Du kannst heute ruhig das Auto nehmen.
du: kanst 'hɔɪtə 'ʁu:ɪç da:s 'aʊto 'ne:mən
you you can today without my objection the car to take

I don't mind if you use the car today.

(258) Bei so einer Kälte fahre ich nicht mit dem Motorrad.
baɪ zo: 'aɪnɐ 'kɛltə 'fa:ʁə ɪç nɪçt mɪt de:m mo'to:ɐˌʁa:t
with such a cold I drive I not with the motorcycle

I don't ride my motorcycle when it is this cold.

(259) Ich glaube nicht, dass du für das Auto so viel Geld bekommst. Das ist nicht realistisch.
ɪç 'glaʊbə nɪçt das du: fy:ɐ da:s 'aʊto zo: fi:l gɛlt bə'kɔmst das ɪst nɪçt ʁea'lɪstɪʃ
I I think not that you for the car so much money you get that it is not realistic

I don't think you'll get that much money for the car. That is not realistic.

(260) Mit dem Humor dieses Komikers kann ich nichts anfangen.
mɪt de:m hu'mo:ɐ 'di:zəs 'ko:mɪkɐs kan ɪç nɪçts 'anˌfaŋən
→ the humor of this comedian I can I ← to get nothing from

I don't understand the humor of this comedian.

(261) Ich verstehe nicht, was ich nicht erklären kann.
ɪç fɛɐ'ʃte:ə nɪçt vas ɪç nɪçt ɛɐ'klɛ:ʁən kan
I I understand not what I not to explain I can

I don't understand what I can't explain.

(262) Ich verstehe nicht, was Sie meinen. Können Sie das bitte in einfacheren Worten wiederholen?
ɪç fɛɐ'ʃte:ə nɪçt vas zi: 'maɪnən 'kœnən zi: da:s 'bɪtə ɪn 'aɪnfaxəʁən 'vɔʁtən vi:dɐ'ho:lən
I I understand not what you you mean you can you that please in simpler words to repeat

I don't understand what you're saying. Can you please say it again more simply?

(263) Ich will keinen Job, der von mir verlangt, dass ich am
  ɪç vɪl ˈkaɪnən dʒɔp deːɐ fɔn miːɐ fɛɐˈlaŋt das ɪç am
  I I want no job that from me it demands that I on the
  Wochenende arbeite.
  ˈvɔxn̩ˌɛndə ˈaʁbaɪtə
  weekend I work

I don't want a job that makes me work on the weekend.

(264) Ich esse jeden Morgen einen Apfel zum Frühstück.
  ɪç ˈɛsə ˈjeːdn̩ ˈmɔʁɡən ˈaɪnən ˈapfl̩ tsʊm ˈfʁyːʃtʏk
  I I eat every morning an apple for breakfast

I eat an apple every day with my breakfast.

(265) Ich trainiere oft und esse viel Gemüse.
  ɪç tʁɛˈniːʁə ɔft ʊnt ˈɛsə fiːl ɡəˈmyːzə
  I I exercise often and I eat a lot of vegetables

I exercise a lot and eat a lot of vegetables.

(266) Ich finde diesen Stuhl sehr unbequem.
  ɪç ˈfɪndə ˈdiːzən ʃtuːl zeːɐ ˈʊnbəˌkveːm
  I I find this chair very uncomfortable

I find this chair to be very uncomfortable.

(267) Ich hatte meinen Reisepass vergessen. Deswegen musste
  ɪç ˈhatə ˈmaɪnən ˈʁaɪzəˌpas fɛɐˈɡɛsn̩ ˈdɛsˌveːɡn̩ ˈmʊstə
  I → my passport ←I had forgotten therefore I had to
  ich schnell nach Hause gehen, um ihn zu holen.
  ɪç ʃnɛl naːx ˈhaʊzə ˈɡeːən ʊm iːn tsu ˈhoːlən
  I quickly home to go in order to→ it ←to to get

I forgot my passport, so I had to quickly go back home to get it.

(268) Ich habe deinen Geburtstag vergessen. Jetzt habe ich ein
  ɪç ˈhaːbə ˈdaɪnən ɡəˈbuːɐtsˌtaːk fɛɐˈɡɛsn̩ jɛtst ˈhaːbə ɪç aɪn
  I → your birthday ←I forgot now I have I a
  ziemlich schlechtes Gewissen.
  ˈtsiːmlɪç ˈʃlɛçtəs ɡəˈvɪsn̩
  pretty bad conscience

I forgot your birthday. I have quite a guilty conscience.

(269) Ich verstehe mich gut mit meiner Schwiegertochter.
  ɪç fɛɐˈʃteːə mɪç ɡuːt mɪt ˈmaɪnɐ ˈʃviːɡɐˌtɔxtɐ
  I I get along well with my daughter-in-law

I get along well with my daughter-in-law.

(270) Ich stehe jeden Morgen um sechs auf.
  ɪç ˈʃteːə ˈjeːdn̩ ˈmɔʁɡn̩ ʊm zɛks aʊf
  I I get up→ every morning at six ←

I get up every morning at six.

(271) Ich mache einmal die Woche den Lebensmitteleinkauf.
  ɪç ˈmaxə ˈaɪnmaːl diː ˈvɔxə deːn ˈleːbnsˌmɪtl̩ˈaɪnˌkaʊf
  I I do once per week the grocery shopping

I go grocery shopping once a week.

(272) Ich habe sehr jung geheiratet.
  ɪç ˈhaːbə zeːɐ jʊŋ ɡəˈhaɪʁaːtət
  I → very young ←I got married

I got married very young.

(273) Ich habe das Visum von der Botschaft bekommen.
  ɪç ˈhaːbə das ˈviːzʊm fɔn deːɐ ˈboːtʃaft bəˈkɔmən
  I → the visa from the embassy ←I got

I got the visa from the embassy.

(274) **Ich habe ein Geschenk für dich. Es liegt auf dem Tisch.**
ɪç ˈhaːbə aɪn gəˈʃɛŋk fyːɐ dɪç ɛs liːkt aʊf deːm tɪʃ
I I have a gift for you it it lies on the table

I got you a gift. It's on the table.

(275) **Ich hatte einen Autounfall. Jetzt muss ich der Versicherung den Schaden melden.**
ɪç ˈhatə ˈaɪnən ˈaʊtoˌʊnfal jɛtst mʊs ɪç deːɐ fɛɐˈzɪçəʁʊŋ
I I had a car accident now I have to I the insurance
deːn ˈʃaːdn ˈmɛldn
the damage to report

I had an accident with the car. Now I have to report the damage to the insurance company.

(276) **Es war sehr schwierig, einen Parkplatz zu finden.**
ɛs vaːɐ zeːɐ ˈʃviːʁɪç ˈaɪnən ˈpaʁkˌplats tsuː ˈfɪndn
it it was very difficult a parking space to to find

I had great difficulty finding a parking space.

(277) **Ich musste lange auf eine Antwort warten. Aber letztlich habe ich die Stelle bekommen.**
ɪç ˈmʊstə ˈlaŋə aʊf ˈaɪnə ˈantvɔʁt ˈvaʁtn ˈaːbɐ ˈlɛtstlɪç
I I had to long time for an answer to wait but in the end
ˈhaːbə ɪç diː ˈʃtɛlə bəˈkɔmən
→ I the job ←I got

I had to wait a long time for an answer. But I got the job in the end.

(278) **Ich hasse den Klang meiner Stimme.**
ɪç ˈhasə deːn klaŋ ˈmaɪnɐ ˈʃtɪmə
I I hate the sound of my voice

I hate how my voice sounds.

(279) **Ich habe ein Loch im Zahn. Ich muss zum Zahnarzt.**
ɪç ˈhaːbə aɪn lɔx ɪm tsaːn ɪç mʊs tsʊm ˈtsaːnˌaʁtst
I I have a hole in the tooth I have to to the dentist

I have a cavity in my tooth. I have to go to the dentist.

(280) **Ich bin erkältet. Ich kann nichts riechen.**
ɪç bɪn ɛɐˈkɛltət ɪç kan nɪçts ˈʁiːçn
I I have a cold I I can nothing to smell

I have a cold. I can't smell anything.

(281) **Ich habe eine harte Woche vor mir. Ich muss jeden Tag Überstunden machen.**
ɪç ˈhaːbə ˈaɪnə ˈhaʁtə ˈvɔxə foːɐ miːɐ ɪç mʊs ˈjeːdn
I I have a hard week ahead of me I have to every
taːk ˈyːbɐˌʃtʊndən ˈmaxn
day to work overtime

I have a difficult week ahead of me. I have to work overtime every day.

(282) **Ich habe ein gutes Verhältnis zu meinen Eltern.**
ɪç ˈhaːbə aɪn ˈguːtəs fɛɐˈhɛltnɪs tsuː ˈmaɪnən ˈɛltɐn
I I have a good relationship to my parents

I have a good relationship with my parents.

(283) **Ich habe gerade viel zu tun. – Dann will ich dich nicht länger stören.**
ɪç ˈhaːbə gəˈʁaːdə fiːl tsuː tuːn dan vɪl ɪç dɪç
I I have right now much to to do then I want I you
nɪçt ˈlɛŋɐ ˈʃtøːʁən
no longer to disturb

I have a lot to do at the moment. - Then I don't want to disturb you any longer.

(284) Ich habe ein Kleinkind daheim und kann nicht acht Stunden am Tag arbeiten. Daher würde ich gerne Teilzeit arbeiten.
I have a small child and can't work eight hours a day. Therefore I would like to work half-days.

(285) Ich habe mich umentschieden. Ich komme doch mit.
I have changed my mind. I am coming with you.

(286) Ich habe mich verletzt. Meine Hand blutet.
I have injured myself. My hand is bleeding.

(287) Ich habe viele schöne Erinnerungen aus meiner Kindheit.
I have many nice memories from my childhood.

(288) Ich habe keine Kraft dafür, abends noch zu trainieren.
I have no energy left for exercise in the evening.

(289) Ich habe zehn Jahre Erfahrung auf diesem Gebiet.
I have ten years of experience in this field.

(290) Ich habe drei Kinder und keine Zeit mehr für meine Hobbys.
I have three kids and have no time anymore for my hobbies.

(291) Ich muss mein Handy aufladen. Der Akku ist leer.
I have to charge my phone. The battery is empty.

(292) Ich habe zwei Exemplare von diesem Buch. Willst du eines?
I have two copies of the book. Do you want one?

(293) **Seit dem Eingriff kann ich meinen Arm nicht mehr bewegen.**
zaɪt deːm ˈaɪngʀɪf kan ɪç ˈmaɪnən aʀm nɪçt meːɐ bəˈveːgn̩
since the operation I can I my arm no longer to move

I haven't been able to move my arm since the operation.

(294) **Ich habe heute noch gar nichts gegessen, ich habe also großen Hunger.**
ɪç ˈhaːbə ˈhɔɪtə nɔx gaːɐ nɪçts gəˈgɛsn̩ ɪç ˈhaːbə ˈalzo ˈgʀoːsn̩ ˈhʊŋɐ
I → today still nothing at all ←I have eaten I I have thus big hunger

I haven't eaten anything all day, so I'm quite hungry.

(295) **Ich habe dich ewig nicht mehr gesehen, aber du hast dich kein bisschen verändert.**
ɪç ˈhaːbə dɪç ˈeːvɪç nɪçt meːɐ gəˈzeːən ˈaːbɐ duː hast dɪç kaɪn ˈbɪsçən fɛɐˈɛndɐt
I → you in ages not anymore ←I have seen but you → not a bit ←you have changed

I haven't seen you in ages, but you haven't changed at all.

(296) **Ich bin mit dem Auto gegen einen großen Baum gekracht. Dem Baum geht's gut, aber mein Auto ist zerstört.**
ɪç bɪn mɪt deːm ˈaʊto ˈgeːgn̩ ˈaɪnən ˈgʀoːsn̩ baʊm gəˈkʀaxt deːm baʊm geːts guːt ˈaːbɐ maɪn ˈaʊto ɪst tsɛɐˈʃtøːɐt
I → with the car against a big tree ←I crashed the tree it is okay but my car it is destroyed

I hit a big tree with my car. The tree is fine, but my car is destroyed.

(297) **Ich hoffe, ihr musstet nicht allzu lange warten.**
ɪç ˈhɔfə iːɐ ˈmʊstət nɪçt ˈaltsuː ˈlaŋə ˈvaʀtn̩
I I hope you you had to not too long to wait

I hope you haven't been waiting long.

(298) **Ich erkannte meine Mutter sofort an ihrer Stimme.**
ɪç ɛɐˈkantə ˈmaɪnə ˈmʊtɐ zoˈfɔʀt an ˈiːʀɐ ˈʃtɪmə
I I recognized my mother immediately by her voice

I immediately recognized my mother by her voice.

(299) **Ich habe mir das Knie verletzt. Jetzt kann ich nicht mehr rennen.**
ɪç ˈhaːbə miːɐ daːs kniː fɛɐˈlɛtst jɛtst kan ɪç nɪçt meːɐ ˈʀɛnən
I → the knee ←I injured myself now I can I no longer to run

I injured my knee. Now I can't run.

(300) **Ich muss nur noch schnell Geld aus dem Geldautomaten holen.**
ɪç mʊs nuːɐ nɔx ʃnɛl gɛlt aʊs deːm ˈgɛltaʊtoˌmaːtn̩ ˈhoːlən
I I have to real quickly money from the ATM to get

I just need to quickly get some cash from the ATM.

(301) Ich kenne mich ein bisschen mit Dinosauriern aus, aber ich bin kein Experte.
ɪç ˈkɛnə mɪç aɪn ˈbɪsçən mɪt dinoˈzaʊʁiɐn aʊs ˈaːbɐ ɪç bɪn kaɪn ɛksˈpɛʁtə
I I know→ a little about dinosaurs ← but I I am no expert

I know a bit about dinosaurs, but I'm not an expert.

(302) Ich habe vor der Prüfung so viel gepaukt. Danach habe ich fast alles wieder vergessen.
ɪç ˈhaːbə foːɐ deːɐ ˈpʁyːfʊŋ zoː fiːl gəˈpaʊkt daˈnaːx ˈhaːbə ɪç fast ˈaləs ˈviːdɐ fɛɐˈgɛsn
I → before the test so much ←I crammed afterwards → I almost everything again ←I forgot

I crammed so much before the exam. Afterwards I forgot almost everything.

(303) Ich habe mein Gepäck in einem Schließfach am Bahnhof gelassen.
ɪç ˈhaːbə maɪn gəˈpɛk ɪn ˈaɪnəm ˈʃliːsfax am ˈbaːnhoːf gəˈlasn
I → my luggage in a locker at the train station ←I left

I left my luggage in a locker at the train station.

(304) Ich höre gerne Volksmusik im Radio.
ɪç ˈhøːʁə ˈgɛʁnə ˈfɔlksmuziːk ɪm ˈʁaːdio
I I listen to gladly folk music on the radio

I like listening to folk music on the radio.

(305) Ich spiele gerne Tennis, Squash und andere Schlägersportarten.
ɪç ˈʃpiːlə ˈgɛʁnə ˈtɛnɪs skvɔʃ ʊnt ˈandəʁə ˈʃlɛːgɐʃpɔʁtaːɐtn
I I play gladly tennis squash and other types of racquet sports

I like playing tennis, squash, and any other racquet sport.

(306) Zum Frühstück esse ich gerne Brot mit Butter und Honig.
tsʊm ˈfʁyːʃtʏk ˈɛsə ɪç ˈgɛʁnə bʁoːt mɪt ˈbʊtɐ ʊnt ˈhoːnɪç
for breakfast I eat I gladly bread with butter and honey

I like to eat bread with honey and butter for breakfast.

(307) Beim Autofahren höre ich gerne Musik.
baɪm ˈaʊtoˌfaːʁən ˈhøːʁə ɪç ˈgɛʁnə muˈziːk
during the car driving I listen to I gladly music

I like to listen to music on the radio while I'm driving.

(308) Im letzten Jahr habe ich fünfzehn Prozent meines Körpergewichts verloren.
ɪm ˈlɛtstən jaːɐ ˈhaːbə ɪç ˈfʏnftseːn pʁoˈtsɛnt ˈmaɪnəs ˈkœʁpɐgəˌvɪçts fɛɐˈloːʁən
in the last year → I fifteen percent of my body weight ←I lost

I lost fifteen percent of my body weight over the last year.

(309) Ich habe meine Schuhe verloren, als ich mit den Füßen im Schlamm versunken bin.
I lost my shoes when my feet sank into the mud.

(310) Ich habe meinen Ehering beim Schwimmen im See verloren.
I lost my wedding ring while swimming in the lake.

(311) Ich liebe meine Familie, obwohl sie mich meistens in den Wahnsinn treibt.
I love my family even though they drive me crazy most of the time.

(312) Ich habe das Zimmer abgemessen. Es hat genau 20 m².
I measured the room. It is exactly 20 m².

(313) Ich habe den Zug verpasst, aber der nächste kommt eh in zwanzig Minuten.
I missed the train, but another one is coming in twenty minutes.

(314) Ich brauche eine gute Handcreme, weil meine Hände so trocken sind.
I need some good hand cream because my hands are so dry.

(315) Ich muss meine Tochter bis drei Uhr von der Schule abholen.
I need to pick up my daughter from school no later than three o'clock.

(316) **Ich muss das Auto zur Reparatur in die Werkstatt bringen.**
ɪç mʊs daːs ˈaʊto tsuːɐ ʁepaʁaˈtuːɐ ɪn diː ˈvɛʁkʃtat ˈbʁɪŋən
I I have to the car for repair into the workshop to bring

I need to take the car into the shop to get fixed.

(317) **Ich kaufe nur Bio-Obst und -Gemüse.**
ɪç ˈkaʊfə nuːɐ ˈbiːo-oːpst ʊnt ɡəˈmyːzə
I I buy only organic fruit and vegetables

I only buy organic fruit and vegetables.

(318) **Ich bin gerade erst angekommen. Hast du was**
ɪç bɪn ɡəˈʁaːdə eːɐst ˈanɡəˌkɔmən hast duː vas
I → only just ←I arrived you have you something

dagegen, wenn ich kurz auf die Toilette gehe, bevor
daˈɡeːɡn̩ vɛn ɪç kʊʁts aʊf diː toˈlɛtə ˈɡeːə bəˈfoːɐ
against it if I quickly to the toilet I go before

wir reden?
viːɐ ˈʁeːdn̩
we we chat

I only just arrived. Do you mind if I use the toilet before we start chatting?

(319) **Ich habe vor, Ende des Jahres in Rente zu gehen.**
ɪç ˈhaːbə foːɐ ˈɛndə dɛs ˈjaːʁəs ɪn ˈʁɛntə tsuː ˈɡeːən
I I plan end of the year to retire

I plan to retire at the end of the year.

(320) **Ich schmiere mir nur Butter aufs Brot.**
ɪç ˈʃmiːʁə miːɐ nuːɐ ˈbʊtɐ aʊfs bʁoːt
I I smear myself only butter on the bread

I put only butter on my bread.

(321) **Obwohl ich so schnell rannte, wie ich konnte, habe ich**
ɔpˈvoːl ɪç zoː ʃnɛl ˈʁantə viː ɪç ˈkɔntə ˈhaːbə ɪç
although I as fast I ran as I I could → I

den Bus verpasst.
deːn bʊs fɛɐˈpast
the bus ←I missed

I ran as fast as I could, but I still missed the bus.

(322) **Ich habe geläutet, aber niemand war zu Hause.**
ɪç ˈhaːbə ɡəˈlɔɪtət ˈaːbɐ ˈniːmant vaːɐ tsuː ˈhaʊzə
I I rang (the bell) but nobody he was at home

I rang the doorbell, but nobody was at home.

(323) **Ich mache die Arbeit trotz des niedrigen Gehalts gerne.**
ɪç ˈmaxə diː ˈaʁbaɪt tʁɔts dɛs ˈniːdʁɪɡən ɡəˈhalts ˈɡɛʁnə
I I do the job despite the low pay gladly

I really enjoy this job, despite the low pay.

(324) **Ich esse sehr gerne japanisch.**
ɪç ˈɛsə zeːɐ ˈɡɛʁnə jaˈpaːnɪʃ
I I eat very gladly Japanese

I really like Japanese cuisine.

(325) **Ich habe überall gesucht, trotzdem kann ich meine**
ɪç ˈhaːbə yːbɐˈal ɡəˈzuːxt ˈtʁɔtsdeːm kan ɪç ˈmaɪnə
I → everywhere ←I have searched yet I can I my

Sonnenbrille nicht finden.
ˈzɔnənˌbʁɪlə nɪçt ˈfɪndn̩
sunglasses not to find

I searched everywhere, but I can't find my sunglasses.

(326) Ich sollte aufräumen, bevor die Gäste kommen.
ɪç 'zɔltə 'aʊfˌʁɔɪmən bə'fo:ɐ di: 'gɛstə 'kɔmən
I I should to tidy up before the guests they arrive

I should clean up before the guests arrive.

(327) Ich bin ausgerutscht, weil der Boden so rutschig war.
ɪç bɪn 'aʊsgəˌʁʊtʃt vaɪl de:ɐ 'bo:dn zo: 'ʁʊtʃɪç va:ɐ
I I slipped because the floor so slippery it was

I slipped because the floor was slippery.

(328) Ich habe unser altes Auto verkauft und ein neues gekauft.
ɪç 'ha:bə 'ʊnzɐ 'altəs 'aʊto fɛɐ'kaʊft ʊnt aɪn 'nɔɪəs gə'kaʊft
I →→ our old car ←I sold and one new ←I bought

I sold our old car and bought a new one.

(329) Ich muss noch meinen Koffer für die Reise packen.
ɪç mʊs nɔx 'maɪnən 'kɔfɐ fy:ɐ di: 'ʁaɪzə 'pakn
I I must still my suitcase for the trip to pack

I still have to pack my suitcase for the trip.

(330) Ich wohne noch bei meinen Eltern.
ɪç 'vo:nə nɔx baɪ 'maɪnən 'ɛltɐn
I I live still with my parents

I still live with my parents.

(331) Ich rede jeden Tag mit meiner Mutter.
ɪç 'ʁe:də 'je:dn ta:k mɪt 'maɪnɐ 'mʊtɐ
I I speak every day with my mother

I talk to my mother every day.

(332) Als ich noch keine Kinder hatte, habe ich vieles mit
als ɪç nɔx 'kaɪnə 'kɪndɐ 'hatə 'ha:bə ɪç 'fi:ləs mɪt
when I still no children I had → I many things with
anderen Augen gesehen.
'andəʁən 'aʊgən gə'ze:ən
different eyes ←I saw

I think about many things differently now than before I had children.

(333) Ich glaube, dass er die Wahrheit sagt, aber ich bin mir
ɪç 'glaʊbə das e:ɐ di: 'va:ɐhaɪt 'za:kt 'a:bɐ ɪç bɪn mi:ɐ
I I think that he the truth he tells but I →
nicht ganz sicher.
nɪçt gants 'zɪçɐ
not completely ←I am sure

I think he is telling the truth, but I'm not completely sure.

(334) Ich glaube, dass ich beim Bewerbungsgespräch einen
ɪç 'glaʊbə das ɪç baɪm bə'vɛɐbʊŋsgəˌʃpʁɛ:ç 'aɪnən
I I think that I during the job interview a
guten Eindruck gemacht habe.
'gu:tən 'aɪnˌdʁʊk gə'ma:xt 'ha:bə
good impression I made

I think I made a good impression at the job interview.

(335) Ich fand den Film gut. Wie fandest du ihn?
ɪç fant de:n fɪlm gu:t vi: 'fandəst du: i:n
I I found the movie good how you found you it

I think the movie was good. What do you think?

(336) Ich dachte, wir könnten zusammen fahren und uns
ɪç 'daxtə viːɐ 'kœntən tsu'zamən 'faːʁən ʊnt ʊns
I I thought we we could together to drive and between us
die Spritkosten teilen.
diː 'ʃpʁɪtˌkɔstn̩ 'taɪlən
the fuel costs to split

I thought that we could drive together and split the cost of gas.

(337) Ich verstehe dich besser, wenn du nicht im Dialekt
ɪç fɛɐ'ʃteːə dɪç 'bɛsɐ vɛn duː nɪçt ɪm diaˈlɛkt
I I understand you better when you not in the dialect
sprichst.
ʃpʁɪçst
you speak

I understand you better when you don't speak in dialect.

(338) Ich war sein Babysitter, als er noch ein Baby war.
ɪç vaːɐ zaɪn 'bɛɪbiˌsɪtɐ als eːɐ nɔx aɪn 'beːbi vaːɐ
I I was his babysitter when he still a baby he was

I used to babysit him when he was a baby.

(339) Ich war arbeitslos, habe aber vor Kurzem Arbeit gefunden.
ɪç vaːɐ 'aʁbaɪtsloːs 'haːbə 'aːbɐ foːɐ 'kʊʁtsəm 'aʁbaɪt gə'fʊndn̩
I I was unemployed → but recently job ←I have found

I used to be unemployed, but I recently got a job.

(340) Ich habe lange in der Stadt gewohnt, aber jetzt wohne
ɪç 'haːbə 'laŋə ɪn deːɐ ʃtat gə'voːnt 'aːbɐ jɛtst 'voːnə
I → for a long time in the city ←I lived but now I live
ich mit meiner Familie in der Vorstadt.
ɪç mɪt 'maɪnɐ fa'miːliə ɪn deːɐ 'foːɐʃtat
I with my family in the suburbs

I used to live in the city, but now I live in the suburbs with my family.

(341) Ich wache normalerweise vor meinem Mann auf.
ɪç 'vaxə nɔʁ'maːlɐvaɪzə foːɐ 'maɪnəm man aʊf
I I wake up→ normally before my husband ←

I usually wake up before my husband.

(342) Ich habe England zum erstem Mal vor fünf Jahren besucht.
ɪç 'haːbə 'ɛŋlant tsʊm 'eːɐstəm maːl foːɐ fʏnf 'jaːʁən bə'zuːxt
I → England for the first time ago five years ←I visited

I visited England for the first time five years ago.

(343) Ich will das schöne Wetter ausnutzen und einen
ɪç vɪl daːs 'ʃøːnə 'vɛtɐ 'aʊsˌnʊtsn̩ ʊnt 'aɪnən
I I want the nice weather to take advantage of and a
langen Spaziergang machen.
'laŋən ʃpa'tsiːɐˌgaŋ 'maxn̩
long to go for a walk

I want to take advantage of the nice weather and go for a long walk.

(344) Ich will alleine sein.
ɪç vɪl a'laɪnə zaɪn
I I want alone to be

I want to be alone.

(345) Ich will die Wohnung gründlich saubermachen, bevor
      ɪç vɪl diː ˈvoːnʊŋ   ˈɡʁʏntlɪç   ˈzaʊbɐˌmaxn̩   bəˈfoːɐ̯
      I   I want the apartment thoroughly   to clean   before
unser Besuch kommt.
ˈʊnzɐ bəˈzuːx kɔmt
our   visitor he arrives

I want to clean the apartment thoroughly before our visitor arrives.

(346) Ich möchte das Hemd in eine kleinere Größe umtauschen.
      ɪç ˈmœçtə   daːs hɛmt   ɪn ˈaɪnə ˈklaɪnəʁə ˈɡʁøːsə ˈʊmˌtaʊʃn̩
      I   I would like the   shirt in a   smaller   size   to exchange
Das hier ist zu weit.
das hiːɐ̯ ɪst tsuː vaɪt
this here it is too big

I want to exchange this shirt for a smaller size. This one is too big.

(347) Ich möchte günstig Urlaub machen. Was haben Sie zu
      ɪç ˈmœçtə   ˈɡʏnstɪç   ˈuːɐ̯laʊp ˈmaxn̩   vas   ˈhaːbn̩ ziː tsuː
      I   I would like inexpensively to go on vacation what you have you to
empfehlen?
ɛmˈpfeːlən
to advise

I want to go on an inexpensive vacation. What do you advise?

(348) Ich war neulich einkaufen und bin einem alten
      ɪç vaːɐ̯ ˈnɔɪlɪç   ˈaɪnˌkaʊfn̩   ʊnt bɪn ˈaɪnəm ˈaltən
      I   →   the other day ←I went shopping and →   an   old
Freund über den Weg gelaufen.
ˈfʁɔɪnt   ˈyːbɐ deːn vɛk ɡəˈlaʊfn̩
friend   ←I ran into

I was at the store the other day and ran into an old friend.

(349) Ich hatte einen Autounfall, aber es war nicht meine Schuld.
      ɪç ˈhatə ˈaɪnən   ˈaʊtoˌʊnfal   ˈaːbɐ ɛs vaːɐ̯ nɪçt ˈmaɪnə ʃʊlt
      I   I had a   car accident   but   it it was not   my   fault

I was in a car accident, but it wasn't my fault.

(350) Ich wollte dich gerade anrufen.
      ɪç ˈvɔltə   dɪç   ɡəˈʁaːdə ˈanˌʁuːfn̩
      I   I wanted   you   just   to call

I was just about to call you.

(351) Ich war mit meiner Stelle nicht zufrieden und
      ɪç vaːɐ̯ mɪt ˈmaɪnɐ   ˈʃtɛlə nɪçt tsuˈfʁiːdn̩ ʊnt
      I   I was with my   job   not   happy   and
habe gekündigt.
ˈhaːbə ɡəˈkʏndɪçt
I quit

I was not happy with my job and quit.

(352) Gestern war ich krank, deshalb war ich nicht im Büro.
      ˈɡɛstɐn   vaːɐ̯ ɪç kʁaŋk   ˈdɛshalp   vaːɐ̯ ɪç nɪçt ɪm byˈʁoː
      yesterday   I was I   sick   therefore I was I   not   in the office

I was sick yesterday, which is why I wasn't in the office.

(353) Es hat mich sehr gefreut, Sie zu sehen. Bitte kommen Sie bald wieder.
ɛs hat mɪç zeːɐ gəˈfʁɔɪt ziː tsuː ˈzeːən ˈbɪtə ˈkɔmən ziː balt ˈviːdɐ
it → me very much ←it pleased you to to see please come back→ soon ←

I was very happy to see you. Please visit again soon.

(354) Ich wiege zu viel. Ich sollte abnehmen.
ɪç ˈviːɡə tsuː fiːl ɪç ˈzɔltə ˈapˌneːmən
I I weigh too much I I should to lose weight

I weigh too much. I should lose weight.

(355) Ich bin in fünf Minuten da.
ɪç bɪn ɪn fʏnf miˈnuːtən daː
I I am in five minutes there

I will be there in five minutes.

(356) Ich kopiere dir die Dateien auf den USB-Stick.
ɪç koˈpiːʁə diːɐ diː daˈtaɪən aʊf deːn uːɛsˈbeːˌstɪk
I I copy for you the files on the flash drive

I will copy the files to the flash drive for you.

(357) Ich werde dir auf jeden Fall helfen. Du kannst auf mich zählen.
ɪç ˈveːɐdə diːɐ aʊf ˈjeːdn̩ fal ˈhɛlfn̩ duː kanst aʊf mɪç ˈtsɛːlən
I I will you definitely to help you you can on me to count

I will definitely help you. You can count on me.

(358) Ich gebe dir noch eine Chance.
ɪç ˈɡeːbə diːɐ nɔx ˈaɪnə ʃãːs
I I give to you another chance

I will give you another chance.

(359) Ich werde ihm nie verzeihen können, was er getan hat.
ɪç ˈveːɐdə iːm niː fɛɐˈtsaɪən ˈkœnən vas eːɐ ɡəˈtaːn hat
I I will him never to forgive to be able what he he did

I will never be able to forgive him for what he did.

(360) In diesem Restaurant werde ich nie wieder essen.
ɪn ˈdiːzəm ʁɛstoˈʁãː ˈveːɐdə ɪç niː ˈviːdɐ ˈɛsn̩
in this restaurant I will I never again to eat

I will never come back to this restaurant.

(361) Ich lasse es nicht zu, dass du mich nochmal so behandelst.
ɪç ˈlasə ɛs nɪçt tsuː das duː mɪç ˈnɔxˌmaːl zoː bəˈhandl̩st
I I allow→ it not ← that you me again like this you treat

I won't let you treat me like this anymore.

(362) Neben der Uni arbeite ich Teilzeit.
ˈneːbn̩ deːɐ ˈʊni ˈaʁbaɪtə ɪç ˈtaɪlˌtsaɪt
alongside the university I work I part-time

I work part-time while also going to university.

(363) Ich hätte gerne mehr Informationen, bevor ich eine Entscheidung treffe.
ɪç ˈhɛtə ˈgɛʁnə meːɐ̯ ɪnfɔʁmaˈtsioːnən bəˈfoːɐ̯ ɪç ˈaɪnə ɛntˈʃaɪdʊŋ ˈtʁɛfə
I I would like more information before I a decision I make

I would like more information before I make a decision.

(364) Ich würde ja gerne kommen, aber ich kann nicht.
ɪç ˈvʏʁdə jaː ˈgɛʁnə ˈkɔmən ˈaːbɐ ɪç kan nɪçt
I I would ! gladly to come but I can not

I would like to come, but unfortunately I can't.

(365) Ich würde gerne etwas essen, bevor wir gehen.
ɪç ˈvʏʁdə ˈgɛʁnə ˈɛtvas ˈɛsn̩ bəˈfoːɐ̯ viːɐ̯ ˈgeːən
I I would like something to eat before we we go

I would like to eat something before we go.

(366) Ich möchte abnehmen. Daher mache ich jetzt eine Diät.
ɪç ˈmœçtə ˈapˌneːmən daˈheːɐ̯ ˈmaxə ɪç jɛtst ˈaɪnə diˈɛːt
I I would like to lose weight therefore I make I now a diet

I would like to lose weight. Therefore I'm going on a diet.

(367) Ich würde lieber im Büro als draußen in der heißen Sonne arbeiten.
ɪç ˈvʏʁdə ˈliːbɐ ɪm byˈʁoː als ˈdʁaʊsn̩ ɪn deːɐ̯ ˈhaɪsn̩ ˈzɔnə ˈaʁbaɪtn̩
I I would rather in the office than outside in the hot sun to work

I would like to work in an office instead of outside under the hot sun.

(368) Wenn ich reich wäre, würde ich eine Weltreise machen.
vɛn ɪç ʁaɪç ˈvɛːʁə ˈvʏʁdə ɪç ˈaɪnə ˈvɛltˌʁaɪzə ˈmaxn̩
if I rich I were I would I a round-the-world trip to do

If I were rich, I would go on a round-the-world trip.

(369) Wenn es regnet, feiern wir einfach bei uns zu Hause, statt im Park.
vɛn ɛs ˈʁeːgnət ˈfaɪɐn viːɐ̯ ˈaɪnfax baɪ ʊns tsuː ˈhaʊzə ʃtat ɪm paʁk
if it rains we party we just at our place instead of in the park

If it rains, we'll just have the party at our house instead of at the park.

(370) Du solltest einen Regenschirm mitnehmen, falls es regnet.
duː ˈzɔltəst ˈaɪnən ˈʁeːgnˌʃɪʁm ˈmɪtˌneːmən fals ɛs ˈʁeːgnət
you you should an umbrella to bring with (you) in case it rains

If it's supposed to rain, then you should bring an umbrella.

(371) Wenn die Erdbeeren verdorben sind, sollte man sie wegwerfen.
vɛn diː ˈeːɐtˌbeːʁən fɛɐˈdɔʁbn zɪnt ˈzɔltə man ziː ˈvɛkˌvɛʁfn
if the strawberries spoiled they are one should one them to throw away

If the strawberries have gone bad, then you should throw them away.

(372) Wenn das Wetter schön ist, könnten wir ein Picknick machen.
vɛn daːs ˈvɛtɐ ʃøːn ɪst ˈkœntən viːɐ aɪn ˈpɪkˌnɪk ˈmaxn
if the weather nice it is we could we to have a picnic

If the weather's nice, we could have a picnic.

(373) Wenn wir uns beeilen, verpassen wir nicht das Spielende.
vɛn viːɐ ʊns bəˈaɪlən fɛɐˈpasn viːɐ nɪçt daːs ˈʃpiːlˌɛndə
if we we hurry we miss we not the end of the game

If we hurry, we can still watch the end of the game.

(374) Wenn man seine Rechnungen nicht rechtzeitig bezahlt, bekommt man eine Mahnung.
vɛn man ˈzaɪnə ˈʁɛçnʊŋən nɪçt ˈʁɛçtˌtsaɪtɪç bəˈtsaːlt bəˈkɔmt man ˈaɪnə ˈmaːnʊŋ
if one one's bills not on time one pays one gets one an overdue notice

If you do not pay the bill on time, you will receive an overdue notice.

(375) Wer betrunken Auto fährt, landet im Gefängnis.
veːɐ bəˈtʁʊŋkn ˈaʊto fɛːɐt ˈlandət ɪm gəˈfɛŋnɪs
who drunk car he drives he lands in the jail

If you drive drunk, you will go to jail.

(376) Sollten Sie noch Fragen haben, wenden Sie sich an den Informationsschalter.
ˈzɔltən ziː nɔx ˈfʁaːgn ˈhaːbn ˈvɛndn ziː zɪç an deːn ɪnfɔʁmaˈtsioːnsˌʃaltɐ
you should you still questions to have turn to the information desk

If you have any questions, go to the information desk.

(377) Wenn man ein niedriges Einkommen hat, zahlt man weniger Steuern.
vɛn man aɪn ˈniːdʁɪgəs ˈaɪnˌkɔmən hat ˈtsaːlt man ˈveːnɪgɐ ˈʃtɔɪɐn
if one a low income one has one pays one less taxes

If you have low income, you only pay a little tax.

(378) Wenn Sie auf diesen Schalter drücken, geht die Tür auf.
vɛn ziː aʊf ˈdiːzən ˈʃaltɐ ˈdʁʏkn geːt diː tyːɐ aʊf
if you on this switch you press it opens→ the door ←

If you press here, the door opens.

(379) Wenn man mehr ausgibt, als man verdient, spart man kein Geld.
If you spend more than you earn, then you won't save any money.

(380) Wenn du die Datei öffnen willst, musst du zweimal mit der Maus darauf klicken.
If you want to open the file you have to click twice with the mouse.

(381) Ich bin gleich wieder da. Das sollte nur ein paar Minuten dauern.
I'll be right back. This should take only a few minutes.

(382) Ich rufe dich heute Abend an.
I'll call you tonight.

(383) Ich schicke dir eine E-Mail, sobald ich wieder Internetzugang habe.
I'll email you when I get there once I have internet access.

(384) Ich hole dir was zu trinken. Du musst ja Durst haben.
I'll get you something to drink. You must be thirsty.

(385) Das gebe ich Ihnen gratis. – Warum? Wo ist der Haken?
I'll give this to you for free. – Why? What's the catch?

(386) Wir treffen uns im Café gegenüber der Schule.
I'll meet you at the café across from the school.

(387) **Ich verkaufe Ihnen die Tomaten zum halben Preis.**
ɪç fɛɐ̯ˈkaʊfə ˈiːnən diː toˈmaːtən tsʊm ˈhalbən pʁaɪs
I I sell to you the tomatoes at half price

I'll sell you the tomatoes for half price.

(388) **Ich schaufle den Schnee in der Einfahrt weg, wenn du**
ɪç ˈʃaʊflə deːn ʃneː ɪn deːɐ̯ ˈaɪnˌfaːɐ̯t vɛk vɛn duː
I I shovel away→ the snow in the driveway ← if you

den Gehsteig freischaufelst.
deːn ˈgeːʃtaɪk ˈfʁaɪʃaʊflst
the sidewalk you shovel clear

I'll shovel the snow out of the driveway if you shovel the sidewalk.

(389) **Ich bringe dich nach Hause.**
ɪç ˈbʁɪŋə dɪç naːx ˈhaʊzə
I I bring you home

I'll take you home.

(390) **Ich werde Ihnen das Geld elektronisch überweisen.**
ɪç ˈveːɐ̯də ˈiːnən daːs gɛlt elɛkˈtʁoːnɪʃ yːbɐˈvaɪzn
I I will to you the money electronically to transfer

I'll transfer the money to you electronically.

(391) **Ich warte im Auto auf dich.**
ɪç ˈvaːɐ̯tə ɪm ˈaʊto aʊf dɪç
I I wait in the car for you

I'll wait for you in the car.

(392) **Ich freue mich schon auf den nächsten Urlaub.**
ɪç ˈfʁɔɪə mɪç ʃoːn aʊf deːn ˈnɛːçstən ˈuːɐ̯ˌlaʊp
I I look forward already to the next vacation

I'm already looking forward to my next vacation.

(393) **Ich mache diesen Sommer ein dreimonatiges Praktikum bei**
ɪç ˈmaxə ˈdiːzən ˈzɔmɐ aɪn ˈdʁaɪˌmoːnatɪɡəs ˈpʁaktikʊm baɪ
I I do this summer a three-month internship at

einer Firma.
ˈaɪnɐ ˈfɪʁma
a company

I'm doing an internship at a company for three months this summer.

(394) **Heute geht's mir besser, aber gestern war ich**
ˈhɔɪtə geːts miːɐ̯ ˈbɛsɐ ˈaːbɐ ˈgɛstɐn vaːɐ̯ ɪç
today it goes for me better but yesterday I was I

sehr schlecht drauf.
zeːɐ̯ ʃlɛçt dʁaʊf
in a very bad mood

I'm feeling better today, but yesterday I was in a really bad mood.

(395) **Ich gehe heute Abend mit meinen Schwestern aus.**
ɪç ˈgeːə ˈhɔɪtə ˈaːbnt mɪt ˈmaɪnən ˈʃvɛstɐn aʊs
I I go out→ tonight with my sisters ←

I'm going out with my sisters tonight.

(396) **Es freut mich, dass alles so gut gelaufen ist.**
ɛs fʁɔɪt mɪç das ˈaləs zoː guːt gəˈlaʊfn ɪst
it it pleases me that everything so well it went

I'm happy that everything went so well.

(397) Ich lerne Portugiesisch, weil ich nach Brasilien reisen will.
ɪç ˈlɛʁnə pɔʁtuˈgiːzɪʃ vaɪl ɪç naːx bʁaˈziːliən ˈʁaɪzn vɪl
I I learn Portuguese because I to Brazil to travel I want

I'm learning Portuguese because I want to travel to Brazil.

(398) Ich lerne Gitarrespielen. Ich übe täglich eine Stunde.
ɪç ˈlɛʁnə giˈtaʁəˌʃpiːlən ɪç ˈyːbə ˈtɛːklɪç ˈaɪnə ˈʃtʊndə
I I learn guitar playing I I practice daily an hour

I'm learning to play guitar. I practice an hour every day.

(399) Ich suche einen Kindersitz für meinen dreijährigen Sohn.
ɪç ˈzuːxə ˈaɪnən ˈkɪndɐˌzɪts fyːɐ ˈmaɪnən ˈdʁaɪjɛːʁɪgn zoːn
I I look for a car seat for my three year old son

I'm looking for a car seat for my three-year-old son.

(400) Ich bin auf der Suche nach einem günstigen Ferienhaus.
ɪç bɪn aʊf deːɐ ˈzuːxə naːx ˈaɪnəm ˈgʏnstɪgən ˈfeːʁiənˌhaʊs
I I am in search of a low-priced vacation home

I'm looking for a low-priced vacation home.

(401) Ich suche einen Gebrauchtwagen. Er darf nicht mehr als 3000 Euro kosten.
ɪç ˈzuːxə ˈaɪnən gəˈbʁaʊxtˌvaːgn eːɐ daʁf nɪçt meːɐ als ˈdʁaɪˌtaʊznt ˈɔɪʁo ˈkɔstn
I I look for a used car it it may not more than 3000 Euro to cost

I'm looking for a used car. It may not cost more than 3000 Euro.

(402) Ich suche eine Wohnung mit drei Schlafzimmern.
ɪç ˈzuːxə ˈaɪnə ˈvoːnʊŋ mɪt dʁaɪ ˈʃlaːfˌtsɪmɐn
I I look for an apartment with three bedrooms

I'm looking for an apartment with three bedrooms.

(403) Ich interessiere mich zwar nicht für Philosophie, aber dafür interessiere ich mich sehr für Physik.
ɪç ɪntəʁɛˈsiːʁə mɪç tsvaːɐ nɪçt fyːɐ filozoˈfiː ˈaːbɐ daˈfyːɐ ɪntəʁɛˈsiːʁə ɪç mɪç zeːɐ fyːɐ fyˈziːk
I I am interested admittedly not in philosophy but for it I am interested very much in physics

I'm not interested in philosophy, but I'm very interested in physics.

(404) Ich bin bis Ende August im Urlaub.
ɪç bɪn bɪs ˈɛndə aʊˈgʊst ɪm ˈuːɐˌlaʊp
I I am until end of August on vacation

I'm on vacation until the end of August.

(405) Ich habe kein Geld mehr. Darf ich mir welches ausleihen?
ɪç ˈhaːbə kaɪn gɛlt meːɐ daʁf ɪç miːɐ ˈvɛlçəs ˈaʊsˌlaɪən
I I have no money anymore may I some to borrow

I'm out of money. May I borrow some?

(406) Ich bin ziemlich nervös. Mein Herz schlägt wie wild.
ɪç bɪn ˈtsiːmlɪç nɛʁˈvøːs maɪn hɛʁts ʃlɛːkt viː vɪlt
I I am quite nervous my heart it beats frenziedly

I'm quite nervous. My heart is pounding.

(407) Ich denke ernsthaft darüber nach, in eine andere Stadt zu ziehen.
    ɪç 'dɛŋkə 'ɛʁnsthaft daˈʁyːbɐ naːx ɪn 'aɪnə 'andəʁə ʃtat tsuː 'tsiːən
    I I think→ seriously about it ← to another city to to move

I'm seriously considering whether I should move to another city.

(408) Ich fange langsam an, die Führungsqualitäten meines Chefs anzuzweifeln.
    ɪç 'faŋə 'laŋˌzaːm an diː 'fyːʁʊŋskvaliˌtɛːtn 'maɪnəs ʃɛfs 'antsuˌtsvaɪfln
    I I start→ slowly ← the leadership skills of my boss to doubt

I'm starting to doubt my boss's leadership skills.

(409) Ich bleibe zu Hause, bis das Paket geliefert wird.
    ɪç 'blaɪbə tsuː 'haʊzə bɪs das paˈkeːt gəˈliːfɐt vɪʁt
    I I stay home until the package it is delivered

I'm staying home until the package is delivered.

(410) Ich bin es gewohnt, früh aufzustehen, weil ich Kinder habe.
    ɪç bɪn ɛs gəˈvoːnt fʁyː 'aʊftsuˌʃteːən vaɪl ɪç 'kɪndɐ 'haːbə
    I → it ←I am used to early to wake up because I kids I have

I'm used to waking up early because I have kids.

(411) Ich arbeite heute von Zuhause aus.
    ɪç 'aʁbaɪtə 'hɔɪtə fɔn tsuˈhaʊzə aʊs
    I I work today from→ home ←

I'm working from home today.

(412) Im Herbst sammeln wir Pilze im Wald.
    ɪm hɛʁpst 'zamln viːʁ 'pɪltsə ɪm valt
    in the autumn we gather we mushrooms in the forest

In autumn we gather mushrooms in the forest.

(413) Beim Schach hat jeder Spieler sechzehn Figuren.
    baɪm ʃax hat 'jeːdɐ 'ʃpiːlɐ 'zɛçtseːn fiˈguːʁən
    in the chess he has each player sixteen pieces

In chess, each player has sixteen pieces.

(414) Im Allgemeinen bin ich mit meinem Job sehr zufrieden.
    ɪm algəˈmaɪnən bɪn ɪç mɪt 'maɪnəm dʒɔp zeːʁ tsuˈfʁiːdn
    generally I am I with my job very satisfied

In general I am very satisfied with my job.

(415) In Island gibt es nur drei warme Tage im Jahr.
    ɪn 'iːslant giːpt ɛs nuːʁ dʁaɪ 'vaʁmə 'taːgə ɪm jaːʁ
    in Iceland there are only three hot days in the year

In Iceland there are only three hot days per year.

(416) In meiner Freizeit lerne ich Geige spielen.
    ɪn 'maɪnɐ 'fʁaɪˌtsaɪt 'lɛʁnə ɪç 'gaɪgə 'ʃpiːlən
    in my free time I learn I violin to play

In my free time I am learning to play the violin.

(417) In meinem Psychologiekurs sitzen mehr Frauen als Männer.
    ɪn 'maɪnəm psyçoloˈgiːˌkʊʁs 'zɪtsn meːʁ 'fʁaʊən als 'mɛnɐ
    in my psychology class they sit more women than men

In my psychology class there are more women than men.

(418) **Um Ihre Stimme abzugeben, gehen Sie bitte in diese Wahlkabine.**
ʊm ˈiːʀə ˈʃtɪmə ˈaptsuˌgeːbn ˈgeːən ziː ˈbɪtə ɪn ˈdiːzə ˈvaːlkaˌbiːnə
in order to / your / vote / to hand in / go / please / into / this / voting booth

In order to vote, please go into this booth.

(419) **Beim Fußball verfügt jede Mannschaft über elf Spieler.**
baɪm ˈfuːsˌbal fɛɐˈfyːkt ˈjeːdə ˈmanʃaft ˈyːbɐ ɛlf ˈʃpiːlɐ
in the / soccer / it has available → / each / team / ← / eleven / players

In soccer, there are eleven players on the field for each team.

(420) **In Spanien ist es üblich, spät abends zu essen.**
ɪn ˈʃpaːniən ɪst ɛs ˈyːplɪç ʃpɛːt ˈaːbnts tsuː ˈɛsn
in / Spain / it is / it / common / late / in the evenings / to / to eat

In Spain it is common to eat late at night.

(421) **Im Sommer sollte man nicht ohne Sonnencreme in die Sonne gehen.**
ɪm ˈzɔmɐ ˈzɔltə man nɪçt ˈoːnə ˈzɔnənˌkʀɛːm ɪn diː ˈzɔnə ˈgeːən
in the / summer / one should / one / not / without / sunscreen / into / the / sun / to go

In the summer you should not go out into the sun without wearing sunscreen.

(422) **Auf diesem Markt kann man günstige Preise aushandeln.**
aʊf ˈdiːzəm maʀkt kan man ˈgʏnstɪgə ˈpʀaɪzə ˈaʊsˌhandln
in / this / market / one can / one / low / prices / to negotiate

In this market you can negotiate and get things cheaper.

(423) **Ist der Ring aus Gold? – Teilweise, er ist vergoldet.**
ɪst deːɐ ʀɪŋ aʊs gɔlt ˈtaɪlvaɪzə eːɐ ɪst fɛɐˈgɔldət
it is / the / ring / made of / gold / sort of / it / it is / gold-plated

Is the ring made of gold? - Sort of, it's gold-plated.

(424) **Ist dein Handy kaputt? Dann schicken wir es zum Hersteller zurück und lassen es reparieren.**
ɪst daɪn ˈhɛndi kaˈpʊt dan ˈʃɪkn viːɐ ɛs tsʊm ˈheːɐʃtɛlɐ tsuˈʀʏk ʊnt ˈlasn ɛs ʀepaˈʀiːʀən
it is / your / cell phone / broken / then / we send back → / we / it / to the / manufacturer / ← / and / we have (done) / it / to repair

Is your cell phone broken? We'll send it back to the manufacturer and have it repaired.

(425) **Geben ist seliger als nehmen.**
ˈgeːbn ɪst ˈzeːlɪgɐ als ˈneːmən
to give / it is / better / than / to receive

It is better to give than to receive.

(426) **Draußen ist es kalt.**
ˈdʀaʊsn ɪst ɛs kalt
outside / it is / it / cold

It is cold outside.

(427) **Es ist genau acht Uhr.**
ɛs ɪst gəˈnaʊ axt uːɐ
it / it is / exactly / eight / o'clock

It is exactly eight o'clock.

(428) **Es ist so dunkel hier drinnen. Wo ist der Lichtschalter?**
ɛs ɪst zoː ˈdʊŋkl̩ hiːɐ ˈdʀɪnən voː ɪst deːɐ ˈlɪçtˌʃaltɐ
it it is so dark here inside where it is the light switch

It is so dark in this room. Where is the light switch?

(429) **Es ist sehr nett von dir, mich mitzunehmen.**
ɛs ɪst zeːɐ nɛt fɔn diːɐ mɪç ˈmɪttsuˌneːmən
it it is very nice of you me to pick up

It is very kind of you to pick me up.

(430) **Es hat gerade zu regnen aufgehört, und jetzt ist ein**
ɛs hat ɡəˈʀaːdə tsuː ˈʀeːɡnən ˈaʊfɡəˌhøːɐt ʊnt jɛtst ɪst aɪn
it → just to to rain ← it stopped and now it is a

Regenbogen zu sehen.
ˈʀeːɡn̩ˌboːɡn̩ tsuː ˈzeːən
rainbow to to see

It just stopped raining, and now there is a rainbow.

(431) **Da es geregnet hat, brauche ich jetzt meinen Garten nicht**
daː ɛs ɡəˈʀeːɡnət hat ˈbʀaʊxə ɪç jɛtst ˈmaɪnən ˈɡaʀtn̩ nɪçt
since it it rained I need I now my garden not

zu bewässern.
tsuː bəˈvɛsɐn
to to water

It rained, so I don't need to water my garden.

(432) **Es gehört viel Mut dazu, ein neues Leben in einem**
ɛs ɡəˈhøːɐt fiːl muːt daˈtsuː aɪn ˈnɔɪəs ˈleːbn̩ ɪn ˈaɪnəm
it it takes → a lot of courage ← a new life in a

fremden Land zu beginnen.
ˈfʀɛmdn̩ lant tsuː bəˈɡɪnən
foreign country to to start

It takes a lot of courage to start a new life in a foreign country.

(433) **Ich brauche ungefähr 10 Minuten bis zur Arbeit.**
ɪç ˈbʀaʊxə ˈʊnɡəfɛːɐ tseːn mɪˈnuːtən bɪs tsuːɐ ˈaʀbaɪt
I I need about ten minutes to the work

It takes me about 10 minutes to drive to work.

(434) **Das Konzert war großartig. Das Publikum war echt**
das kɔnˈtsɛʀt vaːɐ ˈɡʀoːsˌaːɐtɪç das ˈpuːblikʊm vaːɐ ɛçt
the concert it was great the audience it was really

begeistert.
bəˈɡaɪstɐt
enthusiastic

It was a great concert. The audience was really enthusiastic.

(435) **Seltsam, dass mein Bruder noch nicht da ist. Sonst ist**
ˈzɛltzaːm das maɪn ˈbʀuːdɐ nɔx nɪçt daː ɪst zɔnst ɪst
strange that my brother still not here he is usually he is

er immer so pünktlich.
eːɐ ˈɪmɐ zoː ˈpʏŋktlɪç
he always so punctual

It's strange that my brother isn't here yet. He is usually so punctual.

(436) **Hier drinnen ist es stickig. Mach bitte das Fenster auf.**
hiːɐ ˈdʀɪnən ɪst ɛs ˈʃtɪkɪç max ˈbɪtə das ˈfɛnstɐ aʊf
here inside it is it stuffy open → please the window ←

It's stuffy in here. Please open the window.

(437) Ich bin schon seit zwei Stunden wach.
ɪç bɪn ʃoːn zaɪt tsvaɪ ˈʃtʊndn̩ vax
I I am already for two hours awake

I've been awake for two hours already.

(438) Seit gestern habe ich Halsschmerzen.
zaɪt ˈɡɛstɐn ˈhaːbə ɪç ˈhalsˌʃmɛʁtsən
since yesterday I have I sore throat

I've had a sore throat since yesterday.

(439) Diesen Ausdruck habe ich noch nie gehört.
ˈdiːzən ˈaʊsˌdʁʊk ˈhaːbə ɪç nɔx niː ɡəˈhøːɐ̯t
that expression → I never ←I heard of

I've never heard that expression.

(440) Frag einfach meine Freundin. Sie hat immer gute Ideen.
fʁaːk ˈaɪnfax ˈmaɪnə ˈfʁɔɪndɪn ziː hat ˈɪmɐ ˈɡuːtə iˈdeːən
ask just my girlfriend she she has always good ideas

Just ask my girlfriend. She always has good ideas.

(441) Karl ist schon über 60. Aber er ist immer noch sehr fit.
kaʁl ɪst ʃoːn ˈyːbɐ ˈzɛçtsɪç ˈaːbɐ eːɐ̯ ɪst ˈɪmɐ nɔx zeːɐ̯
Karl he is already over sixty but he he is still very
fɪt
fit

Karl is already over 60. But he is still very fit.

(442) Sag mir bitte so bald wie möglich Bescheid.
zaːk miːɐ̯ ˈbɪtə zoː balt viː ˈmøːklɪç bəˈʃaɪt
let me know→ please as soon as possible ←

Let me know as soon as possible, please.

(443) Lass uns auf dem Balkon zu Abend essen.
las ʊns aʊf deːm balˈkõː tsuː ˈaːbnt ˈɛsn̩
let's on the balcony to eat dinner

Let's eat dinner on the balcony.

(444) Schau in die Kamera und lächle!
ʃaʊ ɪn diː ˈkaməʁa ʊnt ˈlɛçlə
look at the camera and smile

Look at the camera and smile!

(445) Schau in beide Richtungen, bevor du die Straße überquerst.
ʃaʊ ɪn ˈbaɪdə ˈʁɪçtʊŋən bəˈfoːɐ̯ duː diː ˈʃtʁaːsə yːbɐˈkveːɐ̯st
look in both directions before you the street you cross

Look both ways before crossing the street.

(446) Es ist normal, auch mal Fehler zu machen.
ɛs ɪst nɔʁˈmaːl aʊx maːl ˈfeːlɐ tsuː ˈmaxn̩
it it is normal sometimes mistakes to to make

Making mistakes is quite normal.

(447) In dieser Gegend leben viele Künstler und Musiker.
ɪn ˈdiːzɐ ˈɡeːɡnt ˈleːbn̩ ˈfiːlə ˈkʏnstlɐ ʊnt ˈmuːzɪkɐ
in this area they live many artists and musicians

Many artists and musicians live in this neighborhood.

(448) Viele Einwanderer kommen aus Indien.
ˈfiːlə ˈaɪnˌvandəʁɐ ˈkɔmən aʊs ˈɪndiən
many immigrants they come from India

Many immigrants come from India.

(449) **Viele Wörter haben mehrere Bedeutungen.**
ˈfiːlə ˈvœʁtɐ ˈhaːbn̩ ˈmeːʁəʁə bəˈdɔɪtʊŋən
many words they have several meanings

Many words have several meanings.

(450) **Marco spricht vier Sprachen.**
ˈmaʁko ʃpʁɪçt fiːɐ ˈʃpʁaːxən
Marco he speaks four languages

Marco speaks four languages.

(451) **Maria ist sehr schlau und sehr gut in Mathe.**
maˈʁiːa ɪst zeːɐ ʃlaʊ ʊnt zeːɐ guːt ɪn ˈmatə
Maria she is very intelligent and very good in math

Maria is very intelligent and is very good at math.

(452) **Kann ich mir dein Ladegerät ausleihen? Mein Akku**
kan ɪç miːɐ daɪn ˈlaːdəɡəˌʁɛːt ˈaʊsˌlaɪən maɪn ˈaku
I can I → your battery charger ←to borrow my battery

ist alle.
ɪst ˈalə
it is used up

May I borrow your phone charger? My battery died.

(453) **Männer und Frauen sind gleichberechtigt – zumindest in**
ˈmɛnɐ ʊnt ˈfʁaʊən zɪnt ˈɡlaɪçbəˌʁɛçtɪçt tsuˈmɪndəst ɪn
men and women they are having equal rights at least in

meinem Land.
ˈmaɪnəm lant
my country

Men and women have equal rights - at least they do in my country.

(454) **Messi ist ein berühmter Fußballspieler.**
ˈmɛsi ɪst aɪn bəˈʁyːmtɐ ˈfuːsbalˌʃpiːlɐ
Messi he is a famous soccer player

Messi is a famous soccer player.

(455) **Michael ist schon seit drei Tagen nicht mehr in der**
ˈmɪçaˌeːl ɪst ʃoːn zaɪt dʁaɪ ˈtaːɡn̩ nɪçt meːɐ ɪn deːɐ
Michael → already for three days not anymore in the

Schule gewesen.
ˈʃuːlə ɡəˈveːzn̩
school ←he has been

Michael has been absent from school for three days.

(456) **Mike hat sich einen Bart wachsen lassen. Jetzt sieht er**
maɪk hat zɪç ˈaɪnən baːɐt ˈvaksn̩ ˈlasn̩ jɛtst ziːt eːɐ
Mike → a beard ←he let grow now he looks→ he

viel älter aus.
fiːl ˈɛltɐ aʊs
much older ←

Mike has a beard now. He looks much older.

(457) **Mo fährt jeden Tag mit dem Motorrad zur Arbeit.**
moː fɛːɐt ˈjeːdn̩ taːk mɪt deːm moˈtoːɐˌʁaːt tsuːɐ ˈaʁbaɪt
Mo he drives every day with the motorcycle to the work

Mo drives his motorcycle to work every day.

(458) Mama hat sich beim Knoblauchschneiden in den Finger geschnitten.
ˈmama hat zɪç baɪm ˈknoːpˌlaʊxˌʃnaɪdn̩ ɪn deːn ˈfɪŋɐ ɡəˈʃnɪtn̩
Mom → during the garlic chopping in the finger ← she cut

Mom cut her finger while chopping garlic.

(459) Am Montag ist Nationalfeiertag.
am ˈmoːnˌtaːk ɪst natsioˈnaːlˌfaɪɐtaːk
on Monday it is national holiday

Monday is a national holiday.

(460) Über zweihundert Gäste kommen auf die Hochzeit.
ˈyːbɐ ˈtsvaɪˌhʊndɐt ˈɡɛstə ˈkɔmən aʊf diː ˈhɔxˌtsaɪt
over two hundred guests they come to the wedding

More than two hundred guests are coming to the wedding.

(461) Die meisten wissen nicht, dass Ärzte normalerweise keine Ernährungsfachleute sind.
diː ˈmaɪstn̩ ˈvɪsn̩ nɪçt das ˈɛːɐtstə nɔʁˈmaːlɐvaɪzə ˈkaɪnə ɛɐˈnɛːʁʊŋsˌfaxlɔɪtə zɪnt
most they know not that doctors usually no nutrition experts they are

Most people don't realize that doctors usually aren't experts in nutrition.

(462) Die meisten Wissenschaftler meinen, dass der Mensch schuld am Klimawandel sei.
diː ˈmaɪstn̩ ˈvɪsn̩ʃaftlɐ ˈmaɪnən das deːɐ mɛnʃ ʃʊlt am ˈkliːmaˌvandl̩ zaɪ
most scientists they think that the human at fault for the climate change he is

Most scientists say climate change is the fault of humans.

(463) Mein Baby weiß, wie man einen Löffel benutzt.
maɪn ˈbeːbi vaɪs viː man ˈaɪnən ˈlœfl̩ bəˈnʊtst
my baby he knows how one a spoon one uses

My baby knows how to use a spoon.

(464) Früher liebte mein Junge dieses Spielzeug, aber jetzt interessiert er sich nicht mehr dafür.
ˈfʁyːɐ ˈliːptə maɪn ˈjʊŋə ˈdiːzəs ˈʃpiːlˌtsɔɪk ˈaːbɐ jɛtst ɪntəʁɛˈsiːɐt eːɐ zɪç nɪçt meːɐ daˈfyːɐ
back then he loved my boy this toy but now he is interested no longer in it

My boy used to love this toy, but he doesn't care about it anymore.

(465) Mein Bruder ist ein sehr ordentlicher Mensch, meine Schwester dagegen ist eine Chaotin.
maɪn ˈbʁuːdɐ ɪst aɪn zeːɐ ˈɔʁdn̩tlɪçɐ mɛnʃ ˈmaɪnə ˈʃvɛstɐ daˈɡeːɡn̩ ɪst ˈaɪnə kaˈoːtɪn
my brother he is a very tidy person my sister in contrast she is a slob

My brother is a very tidy person, while my sister is a slob.

(466) Mein Bruder ist drei Jahre jünger als ich.
maɪn ˈbʁuːdɐ ɪst dʁaɪ ˈjaːʁə ˈjʏŋɐ als ɪç
my brother he is three years younger than me

My brother is three years younger than me.

(467) **Mein Bruder nimmt nie ab, wenn ich anrufe.**
maɪn ˈbʁuːdɐ nɪmt niː ap vɛn ɪç ˈanˌʁuːfə
my brother he answers (phone)→ never ← when I I call

My brother never answers his phone when I call.

(468) **Mein Auto ist nagelneu. Ich habe es erst gestern gekauft.**
maɪn ˈaʊto ɪst ˈnaːglˈnɔɪ ɪç ˈhaːbə ɛs eːɐst ˈgɛstɐn gəˈkaʊft
my car it is brand new I → it just yesterday ←I bought

My car is brand new. I just bought it yesterday.

(469) **Meine Kinder sind sehr fleißig. Sobald sie nach Hause kommen, machen sie ihre Hausaufgaben.**
ˈmaɪnə ˈkɪndɐ zɪnt zeːɐ ˈflaɪsɪç zoˈbalt ziː naːx ˈhaʊzə ˈkɔmən ˈmaxn ziː ˈiːʁə ˈhaʊsaʊfˌgaːbn
my children they are very diligent as soon as they home they come they do they their homework

My children are very diligent. They always do their homework right when they get home.

(470) **Mein Arbeitskollege ist felsenfest davon überzeugt, dass er eine Beförderung verdient hat.**
maɪn ˈaʁbaɪtskɔˌleːgə ɪst fɛlznˈfɛst daˈfɔn yːbɐˈtsɔɪkt das eːɐ ˈaɪnə bəˈfœʁdəʁʊŋ fɛɐˈdiːnt hat
my work colleague → adamantly about it ←he is convinced that he a promotion he has deserved

My colleague strongly believes that he deserves a promotion.

(471) **Meine Tochter nimmt nie meine Ratschläge an.**
ˈmaɪnə ˈtɔxtɐ nɪmt niː ˈmaɪnə ˈʁaːtˌʃlɛːgə an
my daughter she takes on→ never my advice ←

My daughter never wants my advice.

(472) **Meine Tochter kommt nächstes Jahr ins Gymnasium.**
ˈmaɪnə ˈtɔxtɐ kɔmt ˈnɛːçstəs jaːɐ ɪns gʏmˈnaːziʊm
my daughter she comes next year in the high school

My daughter starts high school next year.

(473) **Mein Lieblingsgetränk ist frisch gepresster Orangensaft.**
maɪn ˈliːplɪŋsgəˌtʁɛŋk ɪst fʁɪʃ gəˈpʁɛstɐ oˈʁãːʒnˌzaft
my favorite drink it is freshly squeezed orange juice

My favorite drink is fresh-squeezed orange juice.

(474) **Mein Flug ist wegen schlechter Wetterbedingungen ausgefallen.**
maɪn fluːk ɪst ˈveːgn ˈʃlɛçtɐ ˈvɛtɐbəˌdɪŋʊŋən ˈaʊsgəˌfalən
my flight → because of bad weather conditions ←it was canceled

My flight was canceled because of bad weather.

(475) **Meine Freundin arbeitet als Krankenpflegerin im Altersheim.**
ˈmaɪnə ˈfʁɔɪndɪn ˈaʁbaɪtət als ˈkʁaŋknˌpfleːgəʁɪn ɪm ˈaltɐsˌhaɪm
my girlfriend she works as caregiver in the retirement home

My girlfriend is a caregiver in a retirement home.

(476) **Mein Großvater arbeitet nicht mehr. Er ist in Pension.**
maɪn ˈgʁoːsˌfaːtɐ ˈaʁbaɪtət nɪçt meːɐ eːɐ ɪst ɪn pãˈzioːn
my grandfather he works not anymore he he is retired

My grandfather is not working anymore. He is retired.

(477) Meine Oma kann keine Treppen mehr steigen.
ˈmaɪnə ˈoːma kan ˈkaɪnə ˈtʁɛpən meːɐ ˈʃtaɪɡn̩
my grandma she can no stairs anymore to climb

My grandma can't climb stairs anymore.

(478) Meine Oma ist gerade fünfundachtzig geworden.
ˈmaɪnə ˈoːma ɪst ɡəˈʁaːdə fʏnfʊntˈaxtsɪç ɡəˈvɔʁdn̩
my grandma → just eighty-five ← she became

My grandma just turned 85.

(479) Meine Großmutter hat uns spannende Geschichten aus
ˈmaɪnə ˈɡʁoːsˌmʊtɐ hat ʊns ˈʃpanəndə ɡəˈʃɪçtən aʊs
my grandmother → us interesting stories of

ihrer Jugend erzählt.
ˈiːʁɐ ˈjuːɡn̩t ɛɐˈtsɛːlt
her youth ← she told

My grandmother told us interesting stories of her youth.

(480) Meine Großeltern starben vor vielen Jahren, aber ich kann
ˈmaɪnə ˈɡʁoːsˌʔɛltɐn ˈʃtaʁbn̩ foːɐ ˈfiːlən ˈjaːʁən ˈaːbɐ ɪç kan
my grandparents they died ago many years but I I can

mich noch gut an sie erinnern.
mɪç nɔx ɡuːt an ziː ɛɐˈʔɪnɐn
→ still well → them ← ← to remember

My grandparents died many years ago, but I can still remember them well.

(481) Meine Mutter hat Blumen und Schokolade zum Geburtstag
ˈmaɪnə ˈmʊtɐ hat ˈbluːmən ʊnt ʃokoˈlaːdə tsʊm ɡəˈbuːɐtsˌtaːk
my mother → flowers and chocolate to the birthday

bekommen.
bəˈkɔmən
← she got

My mother got flowers and chocolate for her birthday.

(482) Meine Mutter ist schon seit zwanzig Jahren selbstständig.
ˈmaɪnə ˈmʊtɐ ɪst ʃoːn zaɪt ˈtsvantsɪç ˈjaːʁən ˈzɛlpstʃtɛndɪç
my mother she is already for twenty years self-employed

My mother has been running her own business for twenty years.

(483) Die Familie meiner Mutter ist sehr groß, daher habe ich
diː faˈmiːliə ˈmaɪnɐ ˈmʊtɐ ɪst zeːɐ ɡʁoːs daˈheːɐ ˈhaːbə ɪç
the family of my mother it is very big so I have I

viele Tanten und Onkel.
ˈfiːlə ˈtantn̩ ʊnt ˈɔŋkl̩
many aunts and uncles

My mother's family is very big, so I have many aunts and uncles.

(484) Mein Nachbar zieht nächsten Monat aus. Hast du
maɪn ˈnaxˌbaːɐ tsiːt ˈnɛçstən ˈmoːnat aʊs hast duː
my neighbor he moves out→ next month ← you have you

immer noch Interesse an der Wohnung?
ˈɪmɐ nɔx ɪntəˈʁɛsə an deːɐ ˈvoːnʊŋ
still interest in the apartment

My neighbor is moving out next month. Are you still interested in the apartment?

(485) Meine zweite Tochter ist Ingenieurin.
ˈmaɪnə ˈtsvaɪtə ˈtɔxtɐ ɪst ɪnʒenˈjøːʁɪn
my second daughter she is engineer

My other daughter is an engineer.

(486) **Meine Eltern starben vor vielen Jahren.**
ˈmaɪnə ˈɛltɐn ˈʃtaʁbn foːɐ ˈfiːlən ˈjaːʁən
my parents they died ago many years

My parents died many years ago.

(487) **Mein Reisepass ist nur noch zwei Monate gültig, ich sollte ihn also sofort verlängern lassen.**
maɪn ˈʁaɪzəˌpas ɪst nuːɐ nɔx tsvaɪ ˈmoːnatə ˈɡʏltɪç ɪç ˈzɔltə
my passport it is only still two months valid I I should
iːn ˈalzo zoˈfɔʁt fɛɐˈlɛŋɐn ˈlasn
it thus immediately to have renewed

My passport is valid for only two more months, so I should renew it immediately.

(488) **Meine Geschwister und ich haben insgesamt neun Kinder.**
ˈmaɪnə ɡəˈʃvɪstɐ ʊnt ɪç ˈhaːbn ɪnsɡəˈzamt nɔɪn ˈkɪndɐ
my siblings and I we have in total nine children

My siblings and I have nine children in total.

(489) **Während meine Schwester dunkles Haar hat, habe ich blondes.**
ˈvɛːʁənt ˈmaɪnə ˈʃvɛstɐ ˈdʊŋkləs haːɐ hat ˈhaːbə ɪç
whereas my sister dark hair she has I have I
ˈblɔndəs
blond

My sister has dark hair, whereas I have blond hair.

(490) **Meine Schwester interessiert sich für Politik, aber ich nicht.**
ˈmaɪnə ˈʃvɛstɐ ɪntəʁɛˈsiːɐt zɪç fyːɐ poliˈtiːk ˈaːbɐ ɪç nɪçt
my sister she is interested in politics but I not

My sister is interested in politics, but I am not interested in it.

(491) **Mein Sohn ist sehr groß geworden. Er ist schon größer als ich.**
maɪn zoːn ɪst zeːɐ ɡʁoːs ɡəˈvɔʁdn eːɐ ɪst ʃoːn ˈɡʁøːsɐ
my son → very tall ←he has become he he is already taller
als ɪç
than me

My son has grown a lot. He is already taller than me.

(492) **Mein Sohn ist sehr dünn. Er isst zu wenig.**
maɪn zoːn ɪst zeːɐ dʏn eːɐ ɪst tsuː ˈveːnɪç
my son he is very thin he he eats too little

My son is very thin. He eats too little.

(493) **Mein Sohn kann sehr gut malen. Er hat viel Phantasie.**
maɪn zoːn kan zeːɐ ɡuːt ˈmaːlən eːɐ hat fiːl fantaˈziː
my son he can very well to paint he he has a lot of imagination

My son paints very well. He has a lot of imagination.

(494) **Mein Sohn ist einfach mit dem Auto davongefahren, ohne mich zu fragen.**
maɪn zoːn ɪst ˈaɪnfax mɪt deːm ˈaʊto daˈfɔŋəˌfaːʁən ˈoːnə
my son → simply with the car ←he drove away without
mɪç tsuː ˈfʁaːɡn
me to to ask

My son simply drove away with the car without asking me.

(495) Mein Sohn will Medizin studieren und wie seine Mutter Arzt werden.
maɪn zoːn vɪl mediˈtsiːn ʃtuˈdiːʁən ʊnt viː ˈzaɪnə ˈmʊtɐ aːɐ̯tst ˈveːɐ̯dn
my son he wants medicine to study and like his mother doctor to become

My son wants to study medicine and become a doctor like his mother.

(496) Meine Frau ist im dritten Monat schwanger.
ˈmaɪnə fʁaʊ ɪst ɪm ˈdʁɪtn ˈmoːnat ˈʃvaŋɐ
my wife she is in the third month pregnant

My wife is three months pregnant.

(497) Mein jüngstes Kind ist vier Jahre alt.
maɪn ˈjʏŋstəs kɪnt ɪst fiːɐ̯ ˈjaːʁə alt
my youngest child he is four years old

My youngest child is four years old.

(498) Normalerweise muss ich montags arbeiten, aber heute ausnahmsweise nicht.
nɔʁˈmaːlɐvaɪzə mʊs ɪç ˈmoːnˌtaːks ˈaʁbaɪtn ˈaːbɐ ˈhɔɪtə ˈaʊsnaːmsˌvaɪzə nɪçt
normally I have to I on Mondays to work but today as an exception not

Normally I have to work on Monday, but today is an exception.

(499) Natürlich helfe ich dir. Wir sind immerhin Freunde.
naˈtyːʁlɪç ˈhɛlfə ɪç diːɐ̯ viːɐ̯ zɪnt ˈɪmɐˌhɪn ˈfʁɔɪndə
of course I help I you we we are after all friends

Of course I will help you. You are my friend after all.

(500) Am Sonntag veranstalten wir eine Party. Ich muss noch viel dafür vorbereiten.
am ˈzɔnˌtaːk fɛɐ̯ˈanʃtaltn viːɐ̯ ˈaɪnə ˈpaːɐ̯ti ɪç mʊs nɔx fiːl daˈfyːɐ̯ ˈfoːɐ̯bəˌʁaɪtən
on Sunday we host we a party I I have to still a lot for it to prepare

On Sunday we're having a party. I still have to prepare a lot for it.

(501) Einerseits will ich die Reise machen, andererseits ist sie aber auch zu teuer.
ˈaɪnɐzaɪts vɪl ɪç diː ˈʁaɪzə ˈmaxn ˈandəʁɐzaɪts ɪst ziː ˈaːbɐ aʊx tsuː ˈtɔɪɐ
on the one hand I want I to take the trip on the other hand it is it however also too expensive

On the one hand I would like to take the trip, on the other hand it is too expensive.

(502) Am nächsten Tag haben wir einen Rundgang durch den Hafen gemacht.
am ˈnɛːçstən taːk ˈhaːbn viːɐ̯ ˈaɪnən ˈʁʊntˌɡaŋ dʊʁç deːn ˈhaːfn ɡəˈmaxt
on the next day → we a tour through the harbor ← we did

On the second day we took a tour through the harbor.

(503) Niemand kann sich mehr eine Welt ohne Internet vorstellen.
'ni:mant kan zɪç me:ɐ 'aɪnə vɛlt 'o:nə 'ɪntɐnɛt 'fo:ɐˌʃtɛlən
nobody he can → anymore a world without internet ← to imagine

One can no longer imagine a world without internet.

(504) Von diesem Turm aus hat man einen atemberaubenden Blick auf die Stadt.
fɔn 'di:zəm tʊʁm aʊs hat man 'aɪnən 'a:təmbəˌʁaʊbndən blɪk aʊf di: ʃtat
from → this tower ← one has one a breathtaking view onto the city

One has an amazing view of the city from this tower.

(505) Ursprünglich wollte ich Arzt werden, stattdessen bin ich Zahnarzt geworden.
'u:ɐʃpʁʏŋlɪç 'vɔltə ɪç a:ɐtst 'veːɐdn ʃtat'dɛsn bɪn ɪç 'tsa:nˌaːɐtst gə'vɔʁdn
originally I wanted I doctor to become instead → I dentist ← I became

Originally I wanted to be a doctor, but instead I became a dentist.

(506) Unser Geschäft läuft gut. Unser Umsatz war in diesem Monat höher als im letzten.
'ʊnzɐ gə'ʃɛft lɔɪft gu:t 'ʊnzɐ 'ʊmˌzats va:ɐ ɪn 'di:zəm 'mo:nat 'hø:ɐ als ɪm 'lɛtstən
our business it runs well our revenue it was in this month higher than in the last

Our business is going well. Our revenues were higher this month than last.

(507) Wir haben nur sieben Angestellte in unserem Unternehmen.
vi:ɐ 'ha:bn nu:ɐ 'zi:bn 'angəˌʃtɛltə ɪn 'ʊnzəʁəm ʊntɐ'ne:mən
we we have only seven employees in our company

Our company has only seven employees.

(508) Unser ganzes Haus ist voller Hundehaare.
'ʊnzɐ 'gantsəs haʊs ɪst 'fɔlɐ 'hʊndəˌha:ʁə
our entire house it is full of dog hair

Our dog's hair is all over the house.

(509) Das Kind unseres Freundes ist seit dem Unfall behindert.
das kɪnt 'ʊnzəʁəs 'fʁɔɪndəs ɪst zaɪt de:m 'ʊnfal bə'hɪndɐt
the child of our friend → since the accident ← he is disabled

Our friend's child has been disabled since the accident.

(510) Unser Nachbar ist sehr höflich. Er wünscht uns immer einen guten Morgen.
'ʊnzɐ 'naxˌba:ɐ ɪst ze:ɐ 'hø:flɪç e:ɐ 'vʏnʃt ʊns 'ɪmɐ 'aɪnən 'gu:tən 'mɔʁgn̩
our neighbor he is very polite he he wishes us always a good morning

Our neighbor is very polite. He always says good morning.

(511) Unsere Miete ist sehr hoch, aber dafür ist die Lage gut.
'ʊnzəʁə 'mi:tə ɪst ze:ɐ ho:x 'a:bɐ da'fy:ɐ ɪst di: 'la:gə gu:t
our rent it is very high but for it it is the location good

Our rent is very high, but the location is good.

(512) **Unsere beiden Kinder sind sehr unterschiedlich.**
ˈʊnzəʁə ˈbaɪdn̩ ˈkɪndɐ zɪnt zeːɐ ˈʊntɐˌʃiːtlɪç
our both children they are very different

Our two children are very different from each other.

(513) **Unsere Fenster sind nicht luftdicht. Es zieht andauernd.**
ˈʊnzəʁə ˈfɛnstɐ zɪnt nɪçt ˈlʊftˌdɪçt ɛs tsiːt ˈanˌdaʊɐnt
our windows they are not airtight there is a draft constantly

Our windows are not airtight. There is always a draft.

(514) **Entschuldigung? Was haben Sie gesagt?**
ɛntˈʃʊldɪɡʊŋ vas ˈhaːbn̩ ziː ɡəˈzaːkt
pardon me what → you ← you said

Pardon me? What did you say?

(515) **Paris ist die Hauptstadt Frankreichs.**
paˈʁiːs ɪst diː ˈhaʊptˌʃtat ˈfʁaŋkʁaɪçs
Paris it is the capital of France

Paris is the capital of France.

(516) **Das Parlament hat ein neues Gesetz erlassen.**
das paʁlaˈmɛnt hat aɪn ˈnɔɪəs ɡəˈzɛts ɛɐˈlasn̩
the parliament → a new law ← it has enacted

Parliament has enacted a new law.

(517) **In jedem Land meckert man über das Wetter.**
ɪn ˈjeːdəm lant ˈmɛkɐt man ˈyːbɐ das ˈvɛtɐ
in every country one grumbles one about the weather

People in every country grumble about the weather.

(518) **Picasso ist der wahrscheinlich berühmteste Maler der Welt.**
piˈkaso ɪst deːɐ vaːɐˈʃaɪnlɪç bəˈʁyːmtəstə ˈmaːlɐ deːɐ vɛlt
Picasso he is the probably most famous painter of the world

Picasso is perhaps the most famous painter in the world.

(519) **Heb deine Klamotten vom Boden auf.**
heːp ˈdaɪnə klaˈmɔtən fɔm ˈboːdn̩ aʊf
pick up → your clothes from the floor ←

Pick up your clothes off the floor.

(520) **Bringen Sie mir bitte eine Tasse heiße Schokolade.**
ˈbʁɪŋən ziː miːɐ ˈbɪtə ˈaɪnə ˈtasə ˈhaɪsə ʃokoˈlaːdə
bring to me please a cup (of) hot chocolate

Please bring me a cup of hot chocolate.

(521) **Bitte werfen Sie keine Wertstoffe in den Haushaltsmüll.**
ˈbɪtə ˈvɛʁfn̩ ziː ˈkaɪnə ˈveːɐtˌʃtɔfə ɪn deːn ˈhaʊshaltsˌmʏl
please throw no recyclables in the household garbage

Please do not throw recycling in the normal garbage.

(522) **Störe mich jetzt bitte nicht. Ich muss mich auf die Arbeit konzentrieren.**
ˈʃtøːʁə mɪç jɛtst ˈbɪtə nɪçt ɪç mʊs mɪç aʊf diː ˈaʁbaɪt kɔntsɛnˈtʁiːʁən
disturb me now please not I I have to → on the work ← to concentrate

Please don't disturb me now. I have to concentrate on my work.

(523) **Bitte begeben Sie sich mindestens eine Stunde vor Abflug zum Flughafen.**
ˈbɪtə bəˈgeːbn̩ ziː zɪç ˈmɪndəstn̩s ˈaɪnə ˈʃtʊndə foːɐ̯ ˈapˌfluːk tsʊm ˈfluːkˌhaːfn̩
please make your way at least one hour before takeoff to the airport

Please get to the airport at least one hour before takeoff.

(524) **Bitte begründen Sie Ihre Meinung.**
ˈbɪtə bəˈgʁʏndn̩ ziː ˈiːʁə ˈmaɪnʊŋ
please justify your opinion

Please justify your opinion.

(525) **Bitte klopfen Sie vor dem Eintreten an.**
ˈbɪtə ˈklɔpfn̩ ziː foːɐ̯ deːm ˈaɪnˌtʁeːtn̩ an
please knock→ before the entering ←

Please knock before entering.

(526) **Bitte lesen Sie sich diese Informationen aufmerksam durch.**
ˈbɪtə ˈleːzn̩ ziː zɪç ˈdiːzə ɪnfɔʁmaˈtsioːnən ˈaʊfˌmɛʁkzaːm dʊʁç
please read through→ this information carefully ←

Please read this information carefully.

(527) **Bitte bleiben Sie während des Starts sitzen.**
ˈbɪtə ˈblaɪbn̩ ziː ˈvɛːʁənt dɛs ʃtaʁts ˈzɪtsn̩
please remain seated→ during the takeoff ←

Please remain seated during takeoff.

(528) **Bitte vergessen Sie nicht, die Heizung vor dem Schlafengehen auszuschalten.**
ˈbɪtə fɛɐ̯ˈgɛsn̩ ziː nɪçt diː ˈhaɪtsʊŋ foːɐ̯ deːm ˈʃlaːfn̩ˌgeːən ˈaʊstsuˌʃaltn̩
please forget not the heating before the going to sleep to turn off

Please remember to turn off the heating before you go to sleep.

(529) **Bitte schalten Sie Ihr Handy in den Vibrations- oder Lautlosmodus.**
ˈbɪtə ˈʃaltn̩ ziː iːɐ̯ ˈhɛndi ɪn deːn viˈbʁaːtsioːns ˈoːdɐ ˈlaʊtloːsˌmoːdʊs
please switch your cell phone in the vibration- or silent-mode

Please set your phone to vibrate or silent.

(530) **Wasch dir bitte die Hände, bevor du das Baby auf den Arm nimmst.**
vaʃ diːɐ̯ ˈbɪtə diː ˈhɛndə bəˈfoːɐ̯ duː daːs ˈbeːbi aʊf deːn aʁm nɪmst
wash yourself please the hands before you the baby in the arm you take

Please wash your hands before holding the baby.

(531) **Kartoffeln können auf viele verschiedene Arten zubereitet werden.**
kaʁˈtɔfl̩n ˈkœnən aʊf ˈfiːlə fɛɐ̯ˈʃiːdənə ˈaːʁtn̩ ˈtsuːbəˌʁaɪtət ˈveːɐ̯dn̩
potatoes they can in many different ways to be prepared

Potatoes can be cooked many different ways.

(532) Stell die Milch in den Kühlschrank. Lass sie nicht auf dem Tresen stehen.
Put the milk in the fridge. Don't leave it on the counter.

(533) Lesen Sie den Vertrag, bevor Sie unterschreiben.
Read the contract before signing.

(534) Lesen Sie vor dem Zusammenbauen des Tisches die Aufbauanleitung.
Read the instructions before assembling the table.

(535) Die Wirtschaft hat sich in letzter Zeit wieder erholt.
Recently the economy has picked up again.

(536) Der Glaube ist manchen Leuten sehr wichtig.
Religion is very important to some people.

(537) In dieser Gegend sind die Mieten sehr hoch.
Rents are very high in this area.

(538) Hin und zurück? Nein, nur eine einfache Fahrt, bitte.
Round-trip? No, just one-way please.

(539) Sara hat mit einer Plastikschaufel ihren Eimer mit Sand gefüllt.
Sara filled her bucket with sand using a plastic shovel.

(540) Sara will zwar studieren, aber andererseits will sie sofort Geld verdienen.
Sara indeed wants to study, but on the other hand, she wants to earn money right away.

(541) Wissenschaftler versuchen, ein Heilmittel gegen Krebs zu finden.
ˈvɪsnˌʃaftlɐ fɛɐˈzuːxn̩ aɪn ˈhaɪlˌmɪtl̩ ˈgeːgn̩ kʁɛps tsuː ˈfɪndn̩
scientists they try a cure for cancer to to find

Scientists are trying to find a cure for cancer.

(542) Sollen wir erst einkaufen gehen und dann zusammen kochen? – Ja, klingt gut.
ˈzɔlən viːɐ eːɐst ˈaɪnˌkaʊfn̩ ˈgeːən ʊnt dan tsuˈzamən ˈkɔxn̩ jaː ˈklɪŋt guːt
we should we first to go shopping and then together to cook yes it sounds good

Shall we go grocery shopping and cook together afterwards? - Yes, that sounds good.

(543) Sollen wir mit den Kindern am Sonntag in den Zoo gehen?
ˈzɔlən viːɐ mɪt deːn ˈkɪndɐn am ˈzɔnˌtaːk ɪn deːn tsoː ˈgeːən
we should we with the kids on Sunday in the zoo to go

Shall we go to the zoo with the kids on Saturday?

(544) Sie geht fast jeden Tag im Hallenbad schwimmen.
ziː geːt fast ˈjeːdn̩ taːk ɪm ˈhalənˌbaːt ˈʃvɪmən
she she goes almost every day in the swimming pool to swim

She goes for a swim almost every day in the indoor swimming pool.

(545) Sie ist schon lange Kundin bei mir. Ich habe ihr einen Sonderpreis gemacht.
ziː ɪst ʃoːn ˈlaŋə ˈkʊndɪn baɪ miːɐ ɪç ˈhaːbə iːɐ ˈaɪnən ˈzɔndɐˌpʁaɪs gəˈmaxt
she she is for a long time customer with me I → for her a special price ←I made

She has been my customer for a long time. I gave her a special price.

(546) Sie hat zwei Kinder aus erster Ehe.
ziː hat tsvaɪ ˈkɪndɐ aʊs ˈeːɐstɐ ˈeːə
she she has two children from first marriage

She has two children from her first marriage.

(547) Sie hat ein seltsames Geräusch aus dem Dachboden gehört.
ziː hat aɪn ˈzɛltzaːməs gəˈʁɔɪʃ aʊs deːm ˈdaxˌboːdn̩ gəˈhøːɐt
she → a strange noise from the attic ←she heard

She heard a strange noise in the attic.

(548) Sie sah während der Fahrt durch die Landschaft aus dem Fenster des Zuges.
ziː zaː ˈvɛːʁənt deːɐ faːɐt dʊʁç diː ˈlantʃaft aʊs deːm ˈfɛnstɐ dɛs ˈtsuːgəs
she she looked through→ during the ride ← the countryside out of the window of the train

She looked out the window of the train as it passed through the countryside.

(549) Sie hat viel geredet, aber ihr Mann hat den ganzen Abend
zi: hat fiːl ɡəˈʁeːdət ˈaːbɐ iːɐ man hat deːn ˈɡantsən ˈaːbnt
she → a lot ← she talked but her husband → the whole evening
kein Wort gesagt.
kaɪn vɔʁt ɡəˈzaːkt
not a word ← he said

She talked a lot, but her husband didn't say a word all evening.

(550) Sie hat mir ihren Namen gesagt, aber ich habe ihn
zi: hat miːɐ ˈiːʁən ˈnaːmən ɡəˈzaːkt ˈaːbɐ ɪç ˈhaːbə iːn
she → me her name ← she told but I → it
vergessen.
fɛɐˈɡɛsn
← I forgot

She told me her name, but I forgot it.

(551) Sie arbeitet für eine Firma in Italien, aber ich weiß nicht
zi: ˈaʁbaɪtət fyːɐ ˈaɪnə ˈfɪʁma ɪn iˈtaːliən ˈaːbɐ ɪç vaɪs nɪçt
she she works for a company in Italy but I I know not
mehr, wie sie heißt.
meːɐ viː zi: ˈhaɪst
anymore how it it is called

She works for some company in Italy, but I can't remember the name.

(552) Sollen wir ein Taxi nehmen oder einfach zu Fuß gehen?
ˈzɔlən viːɐ aɪn ˈtaksi ˈneːmən ˈoːdɐ ˈaɪnfax tsuː fuːs ˈɡeːən
we should we a taxi to take or just to walk

Should we take a taxi or just walk?

(553) Das Rauchen ist in den meisten Restaurants verboten.
das ˈʁaʊxn ɪst ɪn deːn ˈmaɪstn ʁɛstoˈʁɑ̃ːs fɛɐˈboːtn
the smoking it is in most restaurants forbidden

Smoking is prohibited in most restaurants.

(554) Solange du Fieber hast, musst du im Bett bleiben.
zoˈlaŋə duː ˈfiːbɐ hast mʊst duː ɪm bɛt ˈblaɪbn
so long as you fever you have you must you in the bed to stay

So long as you have a fever, you must stay in bed.

(555) Soziale Medien wie Facebook und Twitter können
zoˈtsiaːlə ˈmeːdiən viː ˈfeɪsbʊk ʊnt ˈtvɪtɐ ˈkœnən
social media like Facebook and Twitter they can
süchtig machen.
ˈzʏçtɪç ˈmaxn
to be addictive

Social media, such as Facebook and Twitter, is addictive.

(556) Solarzellen wandeln Sonnenlicht in Strom um.
zoˈlaːɐˌtsɛlən ˈvandln ˈzɔnənlɪçt ɪn ʃtʁoːm ʊm
solar cells they convert → sunlight into electricity ←

Solar panels convert sunlight into electricity.

(557) Manche Nachbarn sind unfreundlich, aber die meisten
ˈmançə ˈnaxbaːɐn zɪnt ˈʊnfʁɔɪntlɪç ˈaːbɐ di: ˈmaɪstn
some neighbors they are unfriendly but most
sind nett.
zɪnt nɛt
they are nice

Some of the neighbors are unfriendly, but most are nice.

(558) **Manchmal ist es besser, ein Haus zu mieten, als es zu kaufen.**
ˈmançmaːl ɪst ɛs ˈbɛsɐ aɪn haʊs tsuː ˈmiːtn als ɛs tsuː ˈkaʊfn
sometimes it is it better a house to to rent than it to to buy

Sometimes renting is better than buying a house.

(559) **Sport ist zu neunzig Prozent Körper- und zu zehn Prozent Kopfsache.**
ʃpɔʁt ɪst tsuː ˈnɔɪntsɪç pʁoˈtsɛnt ˈkœʁpɐ ʊnt tsuː tseːn pʁoˈtsɛnt ˈkɔpfˌzaxə
Sport it is to ninety percent physical- and to ten percent mental

Sports are ninety percent physical and ten percent mental.

(560) **Nimm ein paar Sandwiches für die Fahrt mit.**
nɪm aɪn paːɐ ˈzɛntvɪtʃɪs fyːɐ diː faːɐt mɪt
take with you→ a couple sandwiches for the trip ←

Take a couple of sandwiches with you for the trip.

(561) **Lass dir Zeit. Das hat keine Eile.**
las diːɐ tsaɪt das hat ˈkaɪnə ˈaɪlə
take your time that it has no rush

Take your time. There's no rush.

(562) **Talent allein nützt nichts ohne harte Arbeit.**
taˈlɛnt aˈlaɪn ˈnʏtst nɪçts ˈoːnə ˈhaʁtə ˈaʁbaɪt
talent alone it is of no use without hard work

Talent is futile unless you work hard.

(563) **Teheran hat über acht Millionen Einwohner.**
ˈteːhəʁaːn hat ˈyːbɐ axt mɪlˈioːnən ˈaɪnˌvoːnɐ
Tehran it has over eight million residents

Tehran has over eight million residents.

(564) **Erzähl mir alles über deine Japanreise.**
ɛɐˈtseːl miːɐ ˈaləs ˈyːbɐ ˈdaɪnə ˈjaːpanˌʁaɪzə
tell to me everything about your Japan trip

Tell me all about your trip to Japan.

(565) **Sag mir die Wahrheit. Hast du wieder mit dem Rauchen angefangen?**
zaːk miːɐ diː ˈvaːɐhaɪt hast duː ˈviːdɐ mɪt deːm ˈʁaʊxn ˈangəˌfaŋən
tell to me the truth → you again with the smoking ← you have started

Tell me the truth. Have you started smoking again?

(566) **Zehn Prozent der Bevölkerung wurden im Ausland geboren.**
tseːn pʁoˈtsɛnt deːɐ bəˈfœlkəʁʊŋ ˈvʊʁdən ɪm ˈaʊslant ɡəˈboːʁən
ten percent of the population → abroad ← they were born

Ten percent of the population was born abroad.

(567) **Zum Glück hat es an unserem Hochzeitstag nicht geregnet.**
tsʊm ɡlʏk hat ɛs an ˈʊnzəʁəm ˈhɔxtsaɪtsˌtaːk nɪçt ɡəˈʁeːɡnət
thankfully → it on our wedding day not ← it rained

Thankfully it didn't rain on our wedding day.

(568) **Der Kerl ist stark. Er hebt Gewichte und isst viel.**
deːɐ kɛɐl ɪst ʃtaʁk eːɐ ˈheːpt gəˈvɪçtə ʊnt ɪst fiːl
the guy he is strong he he lifts weights and he eats a lot

That guy is strong. He lifts heavy weights and eats a lot.

(569) **Das ist Alex. Er wohnt nebenan.**
das ɪst ˈaːlɛks eːɐ ˈvoːnt neːbnˈan
that it is Alex he he lives next door

That is Alex. He lives next door.

(570) **Das kommt überhaupt nicht in Frage!**
das kɔmt yːbɐˈhaʊpt nɪçt ɪn ˈfʁaːgə
that → totally ←it is out of the question

That is totally out of the question!

(571) **Dieser Laden ist sechs Tage die Woche geöffnet.**
ˈdiːzɐ ˈlaːdn ɪst zɛks ˈtaːgə diː ˈvɔxə gəˈœfnət
that store it is six days per week open

That store is open six days per week.

(572) **Das Gespräch war unheimlich peinlich. Gott sei Dank ist**
das gəˈʃpʁɛːç vaːɐ ˈʊnhaɪmlɪç ˈpaɪnˌlɪç gɔt zaɪ daŋk ɪst
the conversation it was incredibly awkward thank God it is

es vorbei.
ɛs foːɐˈbaɪ
it over

That was a terribly awkward interaction. I'm glad it's over.

(573) **Das war eine peinliche Situation.**
das vaːɐ ˈaɪnə ˈpaɪnˌlɪçə zituaˈtsioːn
that it was an embarrassing situation

That was an embarrassing situation.

(574) **Die Geschichte ist ja abgefahren. Ist das echt so**
diː gəˈʃɪçtə ɪst jaː ˈapgəˌfaːʁən ɪst das ɛçt zoː
the story it is ! crazy → that really like that

passiert?
paˈsiːɐt
←it happened

That's a crazy story. Did it really happen?

(575) **Der Flughafen befindet sich außerhalb der Stadt.**
deːɐ ˈfluːkˌhaːfn bəˈfɪndət zɪç ˈaʊsɐhalp deːɐ ʃtat
the airport it is located outside of the city

The airport is located outside of the city.

(576) **Meine Mama musste mit dem Rettungswagen ins**
ˈmaɪnə ˈmama ˈmʊstə mɪt deːm ˈʁɛtʊŋsˌvaːgn ɪns
my mom she had to (go) with the ambulance to the

Krankenhaus.
ˈkʁaŋknˌhaʊs
hospital

The ambulance took my mom to the hospital.

(577) **Die Wohnung hat einen großen Nachteil. Sie liegt**
diː ˈvoːnʊŋ hat ˈaɪnən ˈgʁoːsn ˈnaːxtaɪl ziː liːkt
the apartment it has one big drawback it it is located

nicht zentral.
nɪçt tsɛnˈtʁaːl
not centrally

The apartment has one main drawback. It is not centrally located.

(578) Das Baby hat so winzige Finger und Zehen!
das 'beːbi hat zoː 'vɪntsɪgə 'fɪŋɐ ʊnt 'tseːən
the baby he has such tiny fingers and toes

The baby has such little fingers and toes!

(579) Die Rechnung ist Ende des Monats fällig.
diː 'ʁɛçnʊŋ ɪst 'ɛndə dɛs 'moːnats 'fɛlɪç
the bill it is end of the month due

The bill is due at the end of the month.

(580) Die Rechnung stimmt nicht. Der Kellner hat einen Fehler gemacht.
diː 'ʁɛçnʊŋ ʃtɪmt nɪçt deːɐ 'kɛlnɐ hat 'aɪnən 'feːlɐ
the bill correct not the waiter → a mistake
gə'maːxt
← he made

The bill is wrong. The waiter made a mistake.

(581) Der Vogel flog in sein Nest.
deːɐ 'foːgl floːk ɪn zaɪn nɛst
the bird it flew in its nest

The bird flew to its nest.

(582) Das Buch erscheint dieses Jahr.
das buːx ɛɐ'ʃaɪnt 'diːzəs jaːɐ
the book it is published this year

The book will be published this year.

(583) Das Buch, das du suchst, steht ganz oben im Regal.
das buːx daːs duː zuːxst ʃteːt gants 'oːbn ɪm ʁe'gaːl
the book that you you look for it stands at the very top on the shelf

The book you're looking for is on the top shelf.

(584) Der Chef ist gerade nicht da. Um diese Zeit ist er normalerweise im Büro.
deːɐ ʃɛf ɪst gə'ʁaːdə nɪçt daː ʊm 'diːzə tsaɪt ɪst eːɐ
the boss he is right now not here at this time he is he
nɔʁ'maːlɐvaɪzə ɪm by'ʁoː
normally in the office

The boss isn't around right now. He is normally in the office at this time.

(585) Das Brot ist frisch und duftet wunderbar.
das bʁoːt ɪst fʁɪʃ ʊnt 'dʊftət 'vʊndɐbaːɐ
the bread it is fresh and it smells wonderful

The bread is fresh and smells wonderful.

(586) Das Auto ist mittlerweile fünfzehn Jahre alt, aber es fährt immer noch gut.
das 'aʊto ɪst mɪtlɐ'vaɪlə 'fʏnftseːn 'jaːʁə alt 'aːbɐ ɛs fɛːɐt
the car it is by now fifteen years old but it it runs
'ɪmɐ nɔx guːt
still well

The car is now fifteen years old, but it still runs well.

(587) Das Auto hat neue Reifen nötig.
das 'aʊto hat 'nɔɪə 'ʁaɪfn 'nøːtɪç
the car it has need of→ new tires ←

The car needs new tires.

(588) Die Kassen sind vorne. Sie müssen sich anstellen.
diː 'kasn zɪnt 'fɔʁnə ziː 'mʏsn zɪç 'anʃtɛlən
the cash registers they are in the front you you have to to get in line

The cash registers are at the front. You have to get in line.

(589) Die Feier ist eine gute Gelegenheit, um unsere Freunde wiederzusehen.
The celebration is a good opportunity to see our friends.

(590) Der Stuhl ist aus Plastik und nicht aus Holz.
The chair is made of plastic, not wood.

(591) Das Kind macht jeden Tag nach dem Mittagessen ein Nickerchen.
The child takes a short nap every day after lunch.

(592) Die Kinder haben sich heute gut benommen.
The children behaved very well today.

(593) Die Stadt kommt für die Hälfte der Kosten dieses Projektes auf.
The city is paying for half of the costs of the project.

(594) Die nächste Notaufnahme liegt nur eine Straße weiter.
The closest emergency room is just one street over.

(595) Der Mantel passt nicht in den Koffer.
The coat won't fit in the suitcase.

(596) Der Kaffee ist sehr stark.
The coffee is very strong.

(597) Die Kaffeemaschine ist ziemlich leicht zu bedienen.
The coffee machine is quite easy to operate.

(598) Die Kommunikation zwischen den Abteilungen läuft gut.
The communication between the departments is good.

(599) Das Unternehmen hat ein neues Produkt entwickelt.
The company developed a new product.

(600) **Das Unternehmen hat viele Mitarbeiter entlassen.**
das ʊntɐˈneːmən hat ˈfiːlə ˈmɪtaʁˌbaɪtɐ ɛntˈlasn
the company → many employees ← they laid off
The company laid off many employees.

(601) **Das Unternehmen bietet seinen Mitarbeitern die Möglichkeit, Sprachkurse zu besuchen.**
das ʊntɐˈneːmən ˈbiːtət ˈzaɪnən ˈmɪtaʁˌbaɪtɐn diː ˈmøːklɪçkaɪt ˈʃpʁaːxˌkʊʁzə tsuː bəˈzuːxn̩
the company it offers its employees the possibility language courses to to attend
The company offers its employees the chance to attend language courses.

(602) **Die Firma erstattet mir die Reisekosten.**
diː ˈfɪʁma ɛɐˈʃtatət miːɐ diː ˈʁaɪzəˌkɔstn̩
the company they refund me the travel costs
The company pays me back for my travel costs.

(603) **Der Betrieb stellt dieses Jahr drei neue Mitarbeiter ein.**
deːɐ bəˈtʁiːp ˈʃtɛlt ˈdiːzəs jaːɐ dʁaɪ ˈnɔɪə ˈmɪtaʁˌbaɪtɐ aɪn
the company it hires → this year three new employees ←
The company will hire three new people this year.

(604) **Die Anmeldefrist für diesen Kurs ist abgelaufen.**
diː ˈanmɛldəˌfʁɪst fyːɐ ˈdiːzən kʊʁs ɪst ˈapgəˌlaʊfn̩
the term of application for this course it has passed
The deadline for registering for this course has passed.

(605) **Der Zahnarzttermin ist erst übermorgen.**
deːɐ ˈtsaːnˌaɐtstteɐˌmiːn ɪst eːɐst ˈyːbɐˌmɔʁgn
the dental appointment it is not until the day after tomorrow
The dentist appointment is not until the day after tomorrow.

(606) **Der Arzt hat mich zwar untersucht, aber er konnte nichts finden.**
deːɐ aːɐtst hat mɪç tsvaːɐ ʊntɐˈzuːxt ˈaːbɐ eːɐ ˈkɔntə nɪçts ˈfɪndn̩
the doctor → me indeed ← he examined but he he could nothing to find
The doctor examined me but couldn't find anything wrong.

(607) **Der Arzt hat mir den Marsch geblasen, weil ich immer fetter werde.**
deːɐ aːɐtst hat miːɐ deːn maʁʃ gəˈblaːzn̩ vaɪl ɪç ˈɪmɐ ˈfɛtɐ ˈveːɐdə
the doctor → me ← he chewed out because I always fatter I am becoming
The doctor laid into me because I'm getting really fat.

(608) **Der Arzt meinte, ich sollte Sport treiben. Schwimmen oder Radfahren zum Beispiel.**
deːɐ aːɐtst ˈmaɪntə ɪç ˈzɔltə ʃpɔʁt ˈtʁaɪbn̩ ˈʃvɪmən ˈoːdɐ ˈʁaːtˌfaːʁən tsʊm ˈbaɪˌʃpiːl
the doctor he said I I should to work out swimming or bicycling for example
The doctor says I have to exercise, for example, swimming or riding a bicycle.

(609) **Die Tür schließt automatisch.**
diː tyːɐ ˈʃliːst aʊtoˈmaːtɪʃ
the door it closes automatically
The door closes automatically.

(610) Die Wirtschaft ist in einer schweren Krise.
diː ˈvɪʁtʃaft ɪst ɪn ˈaɪnɐ ˈʃveːʁən ˈkʁiːzə
the economy it is in a serious crisis

The economy is in a serious crisis.

(611) Der Aufzug ist außer Betrieb.
deːɐ ˈaʊfˌtsuːk ɪst ˈaʊsɐ bəˈtʁiːp
the elevator it is out of order

The elevator is out of order.

(612) Der Notausgang ist gleich neben der Treppe.
deːɐ ˈnoːtaʊsˌɡaŋ ɪst ɡlaɪç ˈneːbn̩ deːɐ ˈtʁɛpə
the emergency exit it is directly next to the stairs

The emergency exit is right here by the stairs.

(613) Die Fabrik verschmutzt den Fluss.
diː faˈbʁiːk fɛɐˈʃmʊtst deːn flʊs
the factory it pollutes the river

The factory pollutes the river.

(614) Der Brand hat viele Häuser zerstört.
deːɐ bʁant hat ˈfiːlə ˈhɔɪzɐ tsɛɐˈʃtøːɐt
the fire → many houses ← it destroyed

The fire destroyed many houses.

(615) Das Feuer wurde schnell gelöscht.
das ˈfɔɪɐ ˈvʊʁdə ʃnɛl ɡəˈlœʃt
the fire → quickly ← it was extinguished

The fire was quickly extinguished.

(616) Der Flug war kurz. Knapp eine Stunde.
deːɐ fluːk vaːɐ kʊʁts knap ˈaɪnə ˈʃtʊndə
the flight it was short barely an hour

The flight was short. Just under an hour.

(617) Die Blumen blühen schon. Der Frühling ist da.
diː ˈbluːmən ˈblyːən ʃoːn deːɐ ˈfʁyːlɪŋ ɪst daː
the flowers they bloom already the spring it is here

The flowers are already blooming. It's spring.

(618) Das Essen und die Unterkunft waren ausgezeichnet.
das ˈɛsn̩ ʊnt diː ˈʊntɐˌkʊnft ˈvaːʁən ˈaʊsɡəˌtsaɪçnət
the food and the accommodation they were excellent

The food and accommodation were excellent.

(619) Das Essen ist mir zu salzig.
das ˈɛsn̩ ɪst miːɐ tsuː ˈzaltsɪç
the food it is for me too salty

The food is too salty for me.

(620) Ausländische Studenten müssen erst einen Sprachkurs
ˈaʊslɛndɪʃə ʃtuˈdɛntən ˈmʏsn̩ eːɐst ˈaɪnən ˈʃpʁaːxˌkʊʁs
foreign students they must first a language course

absolvieren.
apzɔlˈviːʁən
to complete

The foreign students must first complete a language course.

(621) Der Mülleimer ist voll.
deːɐ ˈmʏlˌaɪmɐ ɪst fɔl
the garbage can it is full

The garbage can is full.

(622) Die Mülltonnen versperren den Gehsteig.
 di: ˈmʏlˌtɔnən fɛɐˈʃpɛʁən deːn ˈgeːʃtaɪk
 the garbage bins they block the sidewalk

The garbage bins are blocking the sidewalk.

(623) Der Müll muss heute Abend rausgebracht werden.
 deːɐ mʏl mʊs ˈhɔɪtə ˈaːbnt ˈʁaʊsɡəˌbʁaxt ˈveːɐdn
 the garbage it must tonight to be taken out

The garbage must be taken out tonight.

(624) Die deutsche Übersetzung dieses Buches ist fast so gut wie
 di: ˈdɔɪtʃə yːbɐˈzɛtsʊŋ ˈdiːzəs ˈbuːxəs ɪst fast zoː guːt viː
 the german translation of this book it is nearly as good as

das Original.
 daːs oʁigiˈnaːl
 the original

The German translation of that book is nearly as good as the original.

(625) Das Glas fiel auf den Boden und zerbrach.
 das ɡlaːs fiːl aʊf deːn ˈboːdn ʊnt tsɛɐˈbʁaːx
 the glass it fell to the floor and it broke

The glass fell to the floor and broke.

(626) Die Regierung sollte auf das Volk hören.
 di: ʁeˈɡiːʁʊŋ ˈzɔltə aʊf daːs fɔlk ˈhøːʁən
 the government it should to the people to listen

The government should listen to the people.

(627) Die Regierung wird die Steuern bestimmt bald erhöhen.
 di: ʁeˈɡiːʁʊŋ vɪʁt di: ˈʃtɔʏɐn bəˈʃtɪmt balt ɛɐˈhøːən
 the government it will the taxes surely soon to raise

The government will surely raise taxes soon.

(628) Das Herz ist ein Liebessymbol.
 das hɛʁts ɪst aɪn ˈliːbəszʏmˌboːl
 the heart it is a love symbol

The heart is a symbol of love.

(629) Das Hotelbett war mir zu weich.
 das hoˈtɛlˌbɛt vaːɐ miːɐ tsuː vaɪç
 the hotel bed it was for me too soft

The hotel bed was too soft for me.

(630) Das Hotel liegt ungefähr zehn Meter vom Strand
 das hoˈtɛl liːkt ˈʊnɡəfɛːɐ tseːn ˈmeːtɐ fɔm ʃtʁant
 the hotel it is located about ten meters from the beach

entfernt.
 ɛntˈfɛʁnt
 away

The hotel is located about ten meters from the beach.

(631) Das Haus sieht so aus, als wäre es vor zweihundert
 das haʊs ziːt zoː aʊs als ˈvɛːʁə ɛs foːɐ ˈtsvaɪˌhʊndɐt
 the house it looks→ like ← as though → it ago two hundred

Jahren erbaut worden.
 ˈjaːʁən ɛɐˈbaʊt ˈvɔʁdən
 years ← it had been built

The house looks like it was built two hundred years ago.

(632) Laut der Spielanleitung kommt der Älteste als Erster dran.
The instructions say that the oldest takes the first turn in this game.

(633) Das Internet macht mir die Arbeit viel leichter.
The internet makes my work much easier.

(634) Die Erfindung des Buchdrucks war für die Menschheit sehr bedeutend.
The invention of printing was very important for humankind.

(635) Der Jacke fehlt ein Knopf.
The jacket is missing a button.

(636) Die Jacke ist mir zu eng.
The jacket is too tight on me.

(637) Die Kinder lachten über den dummen Witz.
The kids laughed at the silly joke.

(638) Das Messer schneidet nicht richtig. Du solltest es schärfen.
The knife doesn't cut well. You should sharpen it.

(639) Die Landschaft ist dort sehr hügelig.
The landscape there is very hilly.

(640) Die Wäsche ist immer noch feucht.
The laundry is still damp.

(641) Die Blätter wechseln schon die Farbe.
The leaves are already changing colors.

(642) Die Limonade ist zu süß. Du hast zu viel Zucker reingetan.
The lemonade is too sweet. You added too much sugar.

(643) Je länger ich Arabisch lerne, desto besser verstehe ich es.
je: 'lɛŋɐ ɪç aˈʁaːbɪʃ 'lɛʁnə 'dɛsto 'bɛsɐ fɛɐ̯'ʃteːə ɪç ɛs
the→ longer I Arabic I learn ←the better I understand I it

The longer I learn Arabic, the better I can understand it.

(644) Die Mehrheit der Weltbevölkerung besitzt ein Handy.
diː 'meːɐ̯haɪt deːɐ̯ 'vɛltbəˌfœlkəʁʊŋ bəˈzɪtst aɪn 'hɛndi
the majority of the world population it owns a cell phone

The majority of people in the world own a cell phone.

(645) Die Milch steht im untersten Kühlschrankfach.
diː mɪlç ʃteːt ɪm 'ʊntɐstən 'kyːlʃʁaŋkˌfax
the milk it stands in the lowest refrigerator shelf

The milk is in the fridge on the bottom shelf.

(646) Der Spiegel hängt nicht gerade.
deːɐ̯ 'ʃpiːgl 'hɛŋt nɪçt gəˈʁaːdə
the mirror it hangs not straight

The mirror isn't hanging straight.

(647) Der Berg ist knapp 3000 m hoch.
deːɐ̯ bɛʁk ɪst knap 'dʁaɪˌtaʊznt 'meːtɐ hoːx
the mountain it is almost 3000 meters high

The mountain is almost 3000 m high.

(648) Der Filmstar hat langes, blondes Haar.
deːɐ̯ 'fɪlmˌʃtaːɐ̯ hat 'laŋəs 'blɔndəs haːɐ̯
the movie star she has long blond hair

The movie star has long, blond hair.

(649) Der Film war spitze. Die Schauspieler waren sehr gut.
deːɐ̯ fɪlm vaːɐ̯ 'ʃpɪtsə diː 'ʃaʊʃpiːlɐ 'vaːʁən zeːɐ̯ guːt
the movie it was great the actors they were very good

The movie was great. The actors were very good.

(650) Der Film war sehr langweilig und vorhersehbar.
deːɐ̯ fɪlm vaːɐ̯ zeːɐ̯ 'laŋvaɪlɪç ʊnt foːɐ̯ˈheːɐ̯zeːˌbaːɐ̯
the movie it was very boring and predictable

The movie was very boring and predictable.

(651) Der Film war sehr komisch. Wir mussten oft lachen.
deːɐ̯ fɪlm vaːɐ̯ zeːɐ̯ 'koːmɪʃ viːɐ̯ 'mʊstn̩ ɔft 'laxn̩
the movie it was very funny we we had to often to laugh

The movie was very funny. We laughed a lot.

(652) Die Musik geht mir auf die Nerven.
diː muˈziːk geːt miːɐ̯ aʊf diː 'nɛʁfn̩
the music it gets to me on the nerves

The music is getting on my nerves.

(653) Die nächste Führung beginnt in fünfzehn Minuten.
diː 'nɛːçstə 'fyːʁʊŋ bəˈgɪnt ɪn 'fʏnftseːn miˈnuːtən
the next tour it begins in fifteen minutes

The next tour begins in fifteen minutes.

(654) Die Teilnehmerzahl ist auf 12 beschränkt.
diː 'taɪlneːmɐˌtsaːl ɪst aʊf tsvœlf bəˈʃʁɛŋkt
the number of participants → to 12 ←it is limited

The number of participants is limited to 12.

(655) **Fisch ist das einzige Tier, das ich esse.**
fɪʃ ɪst daːs ˈaɪntsɪɡə tiːɐ daːs ɪç ˈɛsə
fish it is the only animal that I I eat

The only animal I eat is fish.

(656) **Die Operation ist gut verlaufen. Wir können Sie morgen**
diː opəʁaˈtsioːn ɪst ɡuːt fɛɐˈlaʊfn viːɐ ˈkœnən ziː ˈmɔʁɡn
the operation → well ← it went we we can you tomorrow

aus dem Krankenhaus entlassen.
aʊs deːm ˈkʁaŋknˌhaʊs ɛntˈlasn
from the hospital to discharge

The operation went well. We can discharge you tomorrow from the hospital.

(657) **Das Gegenteil von »klein« ist »groß«.**
das ˈɡeːɡntaɪl fɔn klaɪn ɪst ɡʁoːs
the opposite of small it is big

The opposite of "small" is "big".

(658) **Das Original gehört Ihnen. Wir behalten die Kopie.**
das oʁiɡiˈnaːl ɡəˈhøːɐt ˈiːnən viːɐ bəˈhaltn diː koˈpiː
the original it belongs to you we we keep the copy

The original is for you. We keep the copy.

(659) **Das Open-Air-Konzert wird bei Regen abgesagt.**
das ˈoːpn-ɛːɐ-kɔnˈtsɛʁt vɪʁt baɪ ˈʁeːɡn ˈapɡəˌzaːkt
the open air concert → in the case of rain ← it is canceled

The outdoor concert will be canceled if it rains.

(660) **Das Paket liegt zur Abholung auf der Post bereit.**
das paˈkeːt liːkt tsuːɐ ˈapˌhoːlʊŋ aʊf deːɐ pɔst bəˈʁaɪt
the package it is ready → for the pickup at the post office ←

The package is ready for pickup at the post office.

(661) **Die Hose ist zu lang. Kannst du sie kürzen?**
diː ˈhoːzə ɪst tsuː laŋ kanst duː ziː ˈkʏʁtsn
the pants it is too long you can you it to shorten

The pants are too long. Can you make them shorter?

(662) **Hier sind die Leute ein bisschen anders als im Süden.**
hiːɐ zɪnt diː ˈlɔɪtə aɪn ˈbɪsçən ˈandɐs als ɪm ˈzyːdn
here they are the people a little different than in the South

The people are a bit different here than in the South.

(663) **Die Leute flüchten und suchen um Asyl an.**
diː ˈlɔɪtə ˈflʏçtn ʊnt ˈzuːxn ʊm aˈzyːl an
the people they flee and they ask → for asylum ←

The people are fleeing and requesting asylum.

(664) **Die Leute protestieren gegen das Kohlekraftwerk.**
diː ˈlɔɪtə pʁotɛsˈtiːʁən ˈɡeːɡn das ˈkoːləˌkʁaftvɛʁk
the people they protest against the coal-fired power plant

The people are protesting against the coal power plant.

(665) **Die Polizei hat die Waffe gefunden.**
diː poliˈtsaɪ hat diː ˈvafə ɡəˈfʊndn
the police → the weapon ← it found

The police found the weapon.

(666) **Die Polizei hat den Täter endlich gefasst.**
diː poliˈtsaɪ hat deːn ˈtɛːtɐ ˈɛntlɪç ɡəˈfast
the police → the culprit finally ← it caught

The police have finally caught the culprit.

(667) Ich wurde von der Polizei angehalten, weil ich über
ɪç 'vʊʁdə fɔn deːɐ poli'tsaɪ 'angə,haltn vaɪl ɪç 'yːbɐ
I → by the police ←I was stopped because I through
eine rote Ampel fuhr.
'aɪnə 'ʁoːtə 'ampl fuːɐ
a red traffic light I drove

The police stopped me because I drove through a red traffic light.

(668) Das Problem ist nicht schwierig. Die Lösung ist sehr
das pʁo'bleːm ɪst nɪçt 'ʃviːʁɪç diː 'løːzʊŋ ɪst zeːɐ
the problem it is not difficult the solution it is very
einfach.
'aɪnfax
simple

The problem is not difficult. The solution is very simple.

(669) Der Professor ist weltweit bekannt.
deːɐ pʁo'fɛsoːɐ ɪst 'vɛltvaɪt bə'kant
the professor he is worldwide known

The professor is internationally known.

(670) Die Reparatur ist zu teuer. Woanders kriege ich sie
diː ʁepaʁa'tuːɐ ɪst tsuː 'tɔɪɐ vo'andɐs 'kʁiːɡə ɪç ziː
the repair it is too expensive elsewhere I get it done I it
für die Hälfte.
fyːɐ diː 'hɛlftə
for half-price

The repair is too expensive. I can get it done for half elsewhere.

(671) Der Reporter führt gerade ein Interview.
deːɐ ʁe'pɔʁtɐ fyːɐt ɡə'ʁaːdə aɪn 'ɪntɐvjuː
the reporter he conducts currently an interview

The reporter is currently conducting an interview.

(672) Der Reis muss ungefähr 40 Minuten lang kochen.
deːɐ ʁaɪs mʊs 'ʊngəfɛːɐ 'fɪʁtsɪç mi'nuːtən laŋ 'kɔxn
the rice it has to about forty minutes long to cook

The rice has to cook for about 40 minutes.

(673) Der Teppich ist zwei Meter lang und einen Meter breit.
deːɐ 'tɛpɪç ɪst tsvaɪ 'meːtɐ laŋ ʊnt 'aɪnən 'meːtɐ bʁaɪt
the rug it is two meters long and one meter wide

The rug is two meters long and one meter wide.

(674) Je früher wir da sind, desto eher bekommen wir gute
jeː 'fʁyːɐ viːɐ daː zɪnt 'dɛsto 'eːɐ bə'kɔmən viːɐ 'ɡuːtə
the→ sooner we there we are ←the likelier we get we good
Plätze.
'plɛtsə
seats

The sooner we get there, the better our chances of getting a good seat.

(675) Der Herd war noch heiß. Ich habe mich aus Versehen
deːɐ heːɐt vaːɐ nɔx haɪs ɪç 'haːbə mɪç aʊs fɛɐ'zeːən
the stove it was still hot I → myself accidentally
verbrannt.
fɛɐ'bʁant
←I burned

The stove was still hot. I accidentally burned myself.

(676) Die Studentin hat für ihren Vortrag eine gute Note bekommen.
diː ʃtuˈdɛntɪn hat fyːɐ ˈiːʁən ˈfoːɐˌtʁaːk ˈaɪnə ˈguːtə ˈnoːtə bəˈkɔmən.
the student → for her presentation a good grade ← she got

The student got a good grade for her presentation.

(677) Die Schüler dieser Schule tragen einheitliche Uniformen.
diː ˈʃyːlɐ ˈdiːzɐ ˈʃuːlə ˈtʁaːgn̩ ˈaɪnhaɪtlɪçə uniˈfɔʁmən
the students of this school they wear standardized uniforms

The students of this school wear standardized uniforms.

(678) Der Koffer ist viel zu schwer für mich.
deːɐ ˈkɔfɐ ɪst fiːl tsuː ʃveːɐ fyːɐ mɪç
the suitcase it is much too heavy for me

The suitcase is much too heavy for me to carry.

(679) Der Koffer ist sehr leicht. Ich kann ihn selbst tragen.
deːɐ ˈkɔfɐ ɪst zeːɐ laɪçt ɪç kan iːn zɛlpst ˈtʁaːgn̩
the suitcase it is very light I I can it myself to carry

The suitcase is very light. I can carry it alone.

(680) Der Pullover passt mir nicht mehr.
deːɐ pʊˈloːvɐ past miːɐ nɪçt meːɐ
the sweater it fits me no longer

The sweater does not fit me anymore.

(681) Der Lehrer hat mich aufgefordert, die Frage zu beantworten.
deːɐ ˈleːʁɐ hat mɪç ˈaʊfgəˌfɔʁdɐt diː ˈfʁaːgə tsuː bəˈantvɔʁtn̩
the teacher → me ← he called on the question to to answer

The teacher called on me to answer the question.

(682) Der Lehrer hat meine Fehler korrigiert.
deːɐ ˈleːʁɐ hat ˈmaɪnə ˈfeːlɐ kɔʁiˈgiːɐt
the teacher → my mistakes ← he corrected

The teacher corrected my mistakes.

(683) Der Lehrer hat heute viele Hausaufgaben aufgegeben.
deːɐ ˈleːʁɐ hat ˈhɔʏtə ˈfiːlə ˈhaʊsaʊfˌgaːbn̩ ˈaʊfgəˌgeːbn̩
the teacher → today a lot of homework ← he assigned

The teacher gave a lot of homework today.

(684) Der Lehrer hält einen Vortrag über den Zweiten Weltkrieg.
deːɐ ˈleːʁɐ hɛlt ˈaɪnən ˈfoːɐˌtʁaːk ˈyːbɐ deːn ˈtsvaɪtn̩ ˈvɛltˌkʁiːk
the teacher he holds a lecture about the second world war

The teacher is lecturing about the Second World War.

(685) Der Lehrer will, dass wir zwei Buchkapitel noch einmal lesen.
deːɐ ˈleːʁɐ vɪl das viːɐ tsvaɪ ˈbuːxkaˌpɪtl̩ nɔx ˈaɪnmaːl ˈleːzn̩
the teacher he wants that we two book chapters again to read

The teacher said we should re-read two chapters in the book.

(686) Die Erklärung des Lehrers ist besser als die Erklärung im Buch.
diː ɛɐ̯ˈklɛːʁʊŋ dɛs ˈleːʁɐs ɪst ˈbɛsɐ als diː ɛɐ̯ˈklɛːʁʊŋ ɪm buːx
the explanation of the teacher it is better than the explanation in the book

The teacher's explanation is better than the explanation in the book.

(687) Die französische Mannschaft war ein harter Gegner.
diː fʁanˈtsøːzɪʃə ˈmanʃaft vaːɐ̯ aɪ̯n ˈhaʁtɐ ˈɡeːɡnɐ
the French team it was a strong opponent

The team from France was a very strong opponent.

(688) Die Mannschaft hat in dieser Saison nur ein Spiel verloren.
diː ˈmanʃaft hat ɪn ˈdiːzɐ zɛˈzɔ̃ː nuːɐ̯ aɪ̯n ʃpiːl fɛɐ̯ˈloːʁən
the team → in this season only one game ← it lost

The team lost only one game this season.

(689) Die Teekanne ist fast leer. Ich mache uns noch etwas Tee.
diː ˈteːkanə ɪst fast leːɐ̯ ɪç ˈmaxə ʊns nɔx ˈɛtvas teː
the teapot it is almost empty I I make us some more tea

The teapot is almost empty. I'll make us more tea.

(690) Die Temperatur ist ganz plötzlich unter Null gefallen.
diː tɛmpəʁaˈtuːɐ̯ ɪst ɡants ˈplœtslɪç ˈʊntɐ nʊl ɡəˈfalən
the temperature → quite suddenly below zero ← it has fallen

The temperature has quite suddenly fallen below zero.

(691) Der Donner kam zehn Sekunden nach dem Blitz.
deːɐ̯ ˈdɔnɐ kaːm tseːn zeˈkʊndn naːx deːm blɪts
the thunder it came ten seconds after the lightning

The thunder came ten seconds after the lightning.

(692) Das Thema Kindererziehung interessiert mich sehr, da ich schwanger bin.
das ˈteːma ˈkɪndɐɛɐ̯ˌtsiːʊŋ ɪntəʁɛˈsiːɐ̯t mɪç zeːɐ̯ daː ɪç ˈʃvaŋɐ bɪn
the topic parenting it interests me very much because I pregnant I am

The topic of parenting interests me very much because I am pregnant.

(693) Das Touristenvisum ist neunzig Tage gültig.
das tuˈʁɪstn̩ˌviːzʊm ɪst ˈnɔɪ̯ntsɪç ˈtaːɡə ˈɡʏltɪç
the tourist visa it is ninety days valid

The tourist visa is valid for ninety days.

(694) Die Handtücher liegen ganz oben im Regal.
diː ˈhantˌtyːçɐ ˈliːɡn̩ ɡants ˈoːbn̩ ɪm ʁeˈɡaːl
the towels they lie at the very top on the shelf

The towels are on the top shelf.

(695) Die Ampel war kaputt. Ein Polizist musste den Verkehr regeln.
diː ˈampl̩ vaːɐ̯ kaˈpʊt aɪ̯n poliˈtsɪst ˈmʊstə deːn fɛɐ̯ˈkeːɐ̯ ˈʁeːɡln̩
the traffic light it was broken a policeman he had to the traffic to direct

The traffic light was broken. A policeman directed traffic.

(696) **Der Zug kommt in 30 Minuten. Bis dahin können wir uns hinsetzen und quatschen.**
deːɐ tsuːk kɔmt ɪn ˈdʀaɪsɪç miˈnuːtən bɪs daˈhɪn ˈkœnən viːɐ ʊns ˈhɪnˌzɛtsn̩ ʊnt ˈkvatʃn̩
the train it comes in thirty minutes until then we can we to sit down and to chat

The train comes in 30 minutes. Until then, we can sit here and chat.

(697) **Das Universum ist riesengroß.**
das uniˈvɛʀzʊm ɪst ˈʀiːznˈɡʀoːs
the universe it is vast

The universe is very large.

(698) **Die Wände hier sind dünn. Man kann alles hören.**
diː ˈvɛndə hiːɐ zɪnt dʏn man kan ˈaləs ˈhøːʀən
the walls here they are thin one one can everything to hear

The walls are very thin here. You can hear everything.

(699) **Auf der Waschmaschine ist ein Jahr Garantie.**
aʊf deːɐ ˈvaʃmaˌʃiːnə ɪst aɪn jaːɐ ɡaʀanˈtiː
on the washing machine it is one year warranty

The washing machine comes with a one-year warranty.

(700) **Das Rad wurde vor ca. 6000 Jahren erfunden.**
das ʀat ˈvʊʀdə foːɐ ˈtsɪʀka ˈzɛksˌtaʊznt ˈjaːʀən ɛɐˈfʊndn̩
the wheel → ago about 6000 years ← it was invented

The wheel was invented about 6000 years ago.

(701) **Im ganzen Haus riecht es nach frischer Farbe.**
ɪm ˈɡantsən haʊs ʀiːçt ɛs naːx ˈfʀɪʃɐ ˈfaʀbə
in the whole house it smells it of fresh paint

The whole house smells of fresh paint.

(702) **Das Fenster war während des Sturms nicht geschlossen, daher ist viel Regen eingedrungen.**
das ˈfɛnstɐ vaːɐ ˈvɛːʀənt dɛs ʃtʊʀms nɪçt ɡəˈʃlɔsn̩ daˈheːɐ ɪst fiːl ˈʀeːɡn̩ ˈaɪŋəˌdʀʊŋən
the window it was during the storm not closed so → a lot of rain ← it got in

The window was not closed during the storm, so a lot of rain came in.

(703) **Die Arbeiter streiken für höhere Löhne.**
diː ˈaʀbaɪtɐ ˈʃtʀaɪkn̩ fyːɐ ˈhøːəʀə ˈløːnə
the workers they strike for higher wages

The workers are striking for higher wages.

(704) **In dieser Klasse sind 15 Jungen und 10 Mädchen.**
ɪn ˈdiːzɐ ˈklasə zɪnt ˈfʏnftseːn ˈjʊŋən ʊnt tseːn ˈmɛːtçən
in this class there are fifteen boys and ten girls

There are 15 boys and 10 girls in the class.

(705) **Zwischen den Ländern gibt es große kulturelle Unterschiede.**
ˈtsvɪʃn̩ deːn ˈlɛndɐn ɡiːpt ɛs ˈɡʀoːsə kʊltuˈʀɛlə ˈʊntɐʃiːdə
between the countries there are big cultural differences

There are big cultural differences between the countries.

(706) **Das Erlernen von Fremdsprachen bringt viele Vorteile mit sich.**
das ɛɐ̯ˈlɛʁnən fɔn ˈfʁɛmtʃpʁaːxn̩ bʁɪŋt ˈfiːlə ˈfɔɐ̯ˌtaɪ̯lə mɪt zɪç
the acquisition of foreign languages it brings along→ many benefits ←

There are many benefits to learning another language.

(707) **In Paris gibt es viele berühmte Museen.**
ɪn paˈʁiːs giːpt ɛs ˈfiːlə bəˈʁyːmtə muˈzeːən
in Paris there are many famous museums

There are many famous museums in Paris.

(708) **In dieser Gegend gibt es viele Wanderwege.**
ɪn ˈdiːzɐ ˈgeːgn̩t giːpt ɛs ˈfiːlə ˈvandɐˌveːgə
in this area there are many hiking trails

There are many hiking trails in this area.

(709) **In diesem Land gibt es viele gesellschaftliche Probleme.**
ɪn ˈdiːzəm lant giːpt ɛs ˈfiːlə gəˈzɛlʃaftlɪçə pʁoˈbleːmə
in this country there are many social problems

There are many social problems in this country.

(710) **Hühnchen kann man auf viele Arten zubereiten.**
ˈhyːnçən kan man aʊ̯f ˈfiːlə ˈaːɐ̯tn̩ ˈtsuːbəˌʁaɪ̯tn̩
chicken one can one in many ways to prepare

There are many ways to prepare a chicken.

(711) **Es sind keine Verletzungen sichtbar, aber wir sollten das Bein trotzdem untersuchen.**
ɛs zɪnt ˈkaɪ̯nə fɛɐ̯ˈlɛtsʊŋən ˈzɪçtbaːɐ̯ ˈaːbɐ viːɐ̯ ˈzɔltən daːs baɪ̯n ˈtʁɔtsdeːm ʊntɐˈzuːxn̩
there are no injuries visible but we we should the leg anyway to examine

There are no visible injuries, but we should examine the leg anyway.

(712) **Es sind noch Tickets für das Konzert nächste Woche erhältlich.**
ɛs zɪnt nɔx ˈtɪkəts fyːɐ̯ daːs kɔnˈtsɛɐ̯t ˈnɛːçstə ˈvɔxə ɛɐ̯ˈhɛltlɪç
there are still tickets for the concert next week available

There are still tickets available for the concert next week.

(713) **Das Zimmer hat drei Steckdosen.**
das ˈtsɪmɐ hat dʁaɪ̯ ˈʃtɛkˌdoːzn̩
the room it has three power outlets

There are three outlets in this room.

(714) **Es gibt eine Umleitung wegen des Unfalls.**
ɛs giːpt ˈaɪ̯nə ˈʊmˌlaɪ̯tʊŋ ˈveːgn̩ dɛs ˈʊnfals
there is a detour because of the accident

There is a detour because of the accident.

(715) **Es gibt Ermäßigungen für Kinder und Senioren.**
ɛs giːpt ɛɐ̯ˈmɛːsɪgʊŋən fyːɐ̯ ˈkɪndɐ ʊnt zeˈnioːʁən
there is discount for children and seniors

There is a discount for children and seniors.

(716) Von hier aus hat man einen großartigen Blick auf die Stadt.
fɔn hiːɐ aʊs hat man ˈaɪnən ˈgʁoːsˌaːɐtɪgn blɪk aʊf diː ʃtat
from→ here ← one has one a great view onto the city

There is a great view of the city from here.

(717) In den Toiletten ist keine Seife mehr.
ɪn deːn toaˈlɛtn ɪst ˈkaɪnə ˈzaɪfə meːɐ
in the restroom it is no soap anymore

There is no soap in the restroom.

(718) Es ist noch ein bisschen Wein übrig. Willst du noch welchen?
ɛs ɪst nɔx aɪn ˈbɪsçən vaɪn ˈyːbʁɪç vɪlst duː nɔx ˈvɛlçən
it it is still a little wine remaining you want you some more

There is still a bit of wine left. Would you like any more?

(719) Nach dem Essen gab es ein leckeres Dessert.
naːx deːm ˈɛsn gaːp ɛs aɪn ˈlɛkəʁəs dɛˈseːɐ
after the meal there was a delicious dessert

There was a delicious dessert after the meal.

(720) Das sind meine Freunde, also behandle sie bitte nett.
das zɪnt ˈmaɪnə ˈfʁɔɪndə ˈalzo bəˈhandlə ziː ˈbɪtə nɛt
these are my friends so treat them please nicely

These are my friends, so please be nice to them.

(721) In diesen großen Lastwagen werden Waren über weite Strecken transportiert.
ɪn ˈdiːzən ˈgʁoːsn ˈlastˌvaːgn ˈveːɐdn ˈvaːʁən ˈyːbɐ ˈvaɪtə ˈʃtʁɛkn tʁanspɔʁˈtiːɐt
in these big trucks → goods over wide distances ← they are transported

These big trucks are used to transport goods over long distances.

(722) Diese Schmerztabletten sind nur auf Rezept erhältlich.
ˈdiːzə ˈʃmɛʁtstaˌblɛtn zɪnt nuːɐ aʊf ʁeˈtsɛpt ɛɐˈhɛltlɪç
these painkillers they are only by prescription available

These painkillers are available only by prescription.

(723) Sie suchen nach Experten für diese Programmiersprache.
ziː ˈzuːxn naːx ɛksˈpɛɐtn fyːɐ ˈdiːzə pʁogʁaˈmiːɐˌʃpʁaːxə
they they look for experts for this programming language

They are looking for experts in this computer programming language.

(724) Sie sind beide mit meinem Vorschlag einverstanden.
ziː zɪnt ˈbaɪdə mɪt ˈmaɪnəm ˈfoːɐˌʃlaːk ˈaɪnfɐˌʃtandn
they → both with my proposal ← they agreed

They both agreed to my proposal.

(725) Sie konnten sich keine große Hochzeit leisten.
ziː ˈkɔntən zɪç ˈkaɪnə ˈgʁoːsə ˈhɔxˌtsaɪt ˈlaɪstn
they they could → not a big wedding ← to afford

They couldn't afford to pay for a big wedding.

(726) Sie müssen mehr Sport treiben. Sie sollten regelmäßig spazieren gehen.
zi: 'mʏsn meːɐ ʃpɔɐt 'tʁaɪbn zi: 'zɔltən 'ʁeːglˌmɛːsɪç ʃpa'tsiːʁən 'geːən
they they have to more to exercise they they should regularly to go for a walk

They need more exercise. They should go walking regularly.

(727) Dieses Flugzeug fliegt direkt nach New York.
'diːzəs 'fluːkˌtsɔɪk 'fliːkt di'ʁɛkt naːx nju: 'jɔːk
this airplane it flies directly to New York

This airplane flies directly to New York.

(728) Dieses Auto ist das sicherste seiner Klasse.
'diːzəs 'aʊto ɪst daːs 'zɪçɐstə 'zaɪnɐ 'klasə
this car it is the safest of its class

This car is the safest in its class.

(729) Dieser Mantel kostet zwar mehr als der andere, aber er ist es wert.
'diːzɐ 'mantl 'kɔstət tsvaːɐ meːɐ als deːɐ 'andəʁə 'aːbɐ eːɐ ɪst ɛs veːɐt
this coat it costs indeed more than the other but it it's worth it

This coat costs more than that one, but it's worth it.

(730) Diese Zartbitterschokolade enthält nur wenig Zucker.
'diːzə 'tsaːɐtbɪtɐʃokoˌlaːdə ɛnt'hɛlt nuːɐ 'veːnɪç 'tsʊkɐ
this dark chocolate it contains only a little sugar

This dark chocolate contains only a little sugar.

(731) In dieser Schublade befinden sich Papier, Kugelschreiber, Bleistifte und Ähnliches.
ɪn 'diːzɐ 'ʃuːpˌlaːdə bə'fɪndn zɪç pa'piːɐ 'kuːglˌʃʁaɪbɐ 'blaɪˌʃtɪftə ʊnt 'ɛːnlɪçəs
in this drawer there are paper pens pencils and the like

This drawer contains paper, pens, pencils, and other things like that.

(732) Das ist der Personaleingang.
das ɪst deːɐ pɛɐzoˈnaːlaɪnˌgaŋ
this it is the staff entrance

This entrance is for staff only.

(733) Dieses Hotel ist besonders für Familien mit Kindern geeignet.
'diːzəs hoˈtɛl ɪst bəˈzɔndɐs fyːɐ faˈmiːliən mɪt 'kɪndɐn gəˈaɪgnət
this hotel it is particularly for families with children suitable

This hotel is particularly suitable for families with children.

(734) Dieses Haus wurde von einem berühmten Architekten entworfen.
'diːzəs haʊs 'vʊʁdə fɔn 'aɪnəm bəˈʁyːmtən aʁçiˈtɛktən ɛntˈvɔʁfn
this house → by a famous architect ← it was designed

This house was designed by a famous architect.

(735) Dieser Schmuck gehörte meiner Großmutter.
ˈdiːzɐ ʃmʊk ɡəˈhøːɐ̯tə ˈmaɪnɐ ˈɡʁoːsˌmʊtɐ
this jewelry it belonged to my grandmother

This jewelry was my grandmother's.

(736) Diese Arbeit erfordert viel Körperkraft.
ˈdiːzə ˈaʁbaɪt ɛɐ̯ˈfɔʁdɐt fiːl ˈkœɐ̯pɐˌkʁaft
this job it requires a lot of physical strength

This job requires a lot of physical strength.

(737) Dieser Film ist bei Männern beliebter als bei Frauen.
ˈdiːzɐ fɪlm ɪst baɪ ˈmɛnɐn bəˈliːptɐ als baɪ ˈfʁaʊən
this movie it is with men more popular than with women

This movie is more popular among men than women.

(738) Dieser Film ist nur für Erwachsene. Er ist zu brutal für
ˈdiːzɐ fɪlm ɪst nuːɐ̯ fyːɐ̯ ɛɐ̯ˈvaksənə eːɐ̯ ɪst tsuː bʁuˈtaːl fyːɐ̯
this movie it is only for adults it it is too violent for

Kinder.
ˈkɪndɐ
children

This movie is only for adults. It's too violent for children.

(739) Diese Musik ist bei Jugendlichen beliebt.
ˈdiːzə muˈziːk ɪst baɪ ˈjuːɡəntlɪçn̩ bəˈliːpt
this music it is with teenagers popular

This music is popular with teenagers.

(740) Diese Neuigkeit bringt mich auf eine Idee.
ˈdiːzə ˈnɔɪ̯çkaɪt ˈbʁɪŋt mɪç aʊf ˈaɪnə iˈdeː
this piece of news it brings me onto an idea

This new information gives me an idea.

(741) Diese Salbe muss man dreimal täglich auftragen.
ˈdiːzə ˈzalbə mʊs man ˈdʁaɪmaːl ˈtɛːklɪç ˈaʊfˌtʁaːɡn̩
this ointment one must one three times daily to apply

This ointment must be applied three times a day.

(742) Dieses Paket wurde an die falsche Adresse geliefert.
ˈdiːzəs paˈkeːt ˈvʊʁdə an diː ˈfalʃə aˈdʁɛsə ɡəˈliːfɐt
this package → to the wrong address ← it was delivered

This package was delivered to the wrong address.

(743) Dieser Preis gilt nur beim Kauf großer Mengen.
ˈdiːzɐ pʁaɪs ɡɪlt nuːɐ̯ baɪm kaʊf ˈɡʁoːsɐ ˈmɛŋən
this price it applies only with the purchase (of) large quantities

This price is only available if you buy large quantities.

(744) Dieser Bericht hat viele Nachforschungen verlangt.
ˈdiːzɐ bəˈʁɪçt hat ˈfiːlə ˈnaːxˌfɔʁʃʊŋən fɛɐ̯ˈlaŋt
this report → a lot of research ← it required

This report required a lot of research.

(745) Dieser Fluss mündet ins Mittelmeer.
ˈdiːzɐ flʊs ˈmʏndət ɪns ˈmɪtl̩ˌmeːɐ̯
this river it flows into the Mediterranean Sea

This river flows into the Mediterranean Sea.

(746) Dieses Schiff überquert den Atlantischen Ozean zweimal
ˈdiːzəs ʃɪf yːbɐˈkveːɐ̯t deːn atˈlantɪʃən ˈoːtseaːn ˈtsvaɪmaːl
this ship it crosses the Atlantic Ocean twice

im Monat.
ɪm ˈmoːnat
per month

This ship crosses the Atlantic Ocean twice per month.

(747) Dieses Hemd ist nicht in meiner Größe. Es ist viel zu weit.
'di:zəs hɛmt ɪst nɪçt ɪn 'maɪnɐ 'gʁø:sə ɛs ɪst fi:l tsu: vaɪt
this shirt it is not in my size it it is much too wide

This shirt is not the right size for me. It's way too big.

(748) Dieses Lied ist sehr bekannt.
'di:zəs li:t ɪst ze:ɐ bə'kant
this song it is very well-known

This song is very well known.

(749) Diese Geschichte ist sehr berühmt. Du musst sie einfach lesen.
'di:zə gə'ʃɪçtə ɪst ze:ɐ bə'ʁy:mt du: mʊst zi: 'aɪnfax 'le:zn
this story it is very famous you you have to it just to read

This story is very famous. You have to read it.

(750) Diese Sonnencreme hat einen hohen Lichtschutzfaktor (LSF).
'di:zə 'zɔnən‿kʁɛ:m hat 'aɪnən 'ho:ən 'lɪçtʃʊts‿faktoːɐ
this sunscreen it has a high sun protection factor (SPF)

This sunscreen has a high sun protection factor (SPF).

(751) Dieser Pullover ist aus reiner Wolle.
'di:zɐ pʊ'lo:vɐ ɪst aʊs 'ʁaɪnɐ 'vɔlə
this sweater it is made of pure wool

This sweater is made of pure wool.

(752) Dieser Tee muss 5 Minuten in kochend heißem Wasser ziehen.
'di:zɐ te: mʊs fʏnf mi'nu:tən ɪn 'kɔxnt 'haɪsəm 'vasɐ 'tsi:ən
this tea it must five minutes in boiling hot water to steep

This tea should be steeped for 5 minutes in boiling water.

(753) Diesmal möchte ich meinen Urlaub auf einer Insel verbringen.
'di:sma:l 'mœçtə ɪç 'maɪnən 'u:ɐ‿laʊp aʊf 'aɪnɐ 'ɪnzl fɛɐ'bʁɪŋən
this time I would like I my vacation on an island to spend

This time I would like to go to an island for vacation.

(754) Dieser Zug erreicht eine Geschwindigkeit von 200 km/h.
'di:zɐ tsu:k ɛɐ'ʁaɪçt 'aɪnə gə'ʃvɪndɪçkaɪt fɔn 'tsvaɪ‿hʊndɐt 'kilometər pʁo: 'ʃtʊndə
this train it reaches a speed of 200 kilometer per hour

This train reaches a speed of 200 km/h.

(755) **Dieser Impfstoff schützt vor Grippe.**
'diːzɐ 'ɪmpfʃtɔf ʃʏtst foːɐ 'ɡʁɪpə
this vaccine it protects against flu

This vaccine protects against flu.

(756) **Tausende Menschen haben sich versammelt, um die Rede des Präsidenten zu hören.**
'taʊzndə 'mɛnʃən 'haːbn zɪç fɛɐ'zamlt ʊm diː 'ʁeːdə dɛs pʁɛzi'dɛntən tsuː 'høːʁən
thousands of people they gathered in order to → the speech of the president ← to hear

Thousands of people gathered to hear the president's speech.

(757) **Um das Wort zu markieren, klicken Sie einfach zweimal mit der linken Maustaste darauf.**
ʊm daːs vɔʁt tsuː maʁ'kiːʁən 'klɪkn ziː 'aɪnfax 'tsvaɪmaːl mɪt deːɐ 'lɪŋkn 'maʊsˌtastə daˈʁaʊf
in order to → the word ← to highlight click simply twice with the left mouse button on it

To highlight the word, simply double-click with the left mouse button.

(758) **Heute ist Montag, gestern war Sonntag und morgen ist Dienstag.**
'hɔʏtə ɪst 'moːnˌtaːk 'ɡɛstɐn vaːɐ 'zɔnˌtaːk ʊnt 'mɔʁɡn ɪst 'diːnsˌtaːk
today it is Monday yesterday it was Sunday and tomorrow it is Tuesday

Today is Monday, yesterday was Sunday, and tomorrow is Tuesday.

(759) **Die Computer von heute leisten viel mehr als noch vor einem Jahrzehnt.**
diː kɔm'pjuːtɐ fɔn 'hɔʏtə 'laɪstn fiːl meːɐ als nɔx foːɐ 'aɪnəm jaːɐˈtseːnt
the computers of today they accomplish much more than even ago a decade

Today's computers can do much more than a decade ago.

(760) **Morgen habe ich Geburtstag. – Wie alt wirst du?**
'mɔʁɡn 'haːbə ɪç ɡə'buːɐtsˌtaːk viː alt vɪʁst duː
tomorrow I have I birthday how old you become you

Tomorrow is my birthday. – How old will you be?

(761) **Man sollte versuchen, mindestens zwanzig Prozent seines Gehaltes beiseitezulegen.**
man 'zɔltə fɛɐ'zuːxn 'mɪndəstns 'tsvantsɪç pʁo'tsɛnt 'zaɪnəs ɡə'haltəs baɪ'zaɪtətsuˌleːɡn
one one should to try at least twenty percent of one's salary to save

Try to save at least twenty percent of your salary.

(762) **An der nächsten Kreuzung links abbiegen.**
an deːɐ 'nɛːçstən 'kʁɔʏtsʊŋ lɪŋks 'apˌbiːɡn
at the next intersection to turn left

Turn left at the next intersection.

(763) **Schalten Sie ihr Handy aus, bevor der Film anfängt.**
'ʃaltən ziː iːɐ 'hɛndi aʊs bə'foːɐ deːɐ fɪlm 'anˌfɛŋt
turn off → your cell phone ← before the movie it starts

Turn off your cell phone before the movie starts.

(764) Leider kann er das Essen nicht genießen, weil es zu scharf ist.
ˈlaɪdɐ kan eːɐ daːs ˈɛsn nɪçt gəˈniːsn vaɪl ɛs tsuː ʃaʁf ɪst
unfortunately he can he the food not to enjoy because it too spicy it is

Unfortunately he can't enjoy the food because it is too spicy.

(765) Mein Fahrrad ist leider kaputtgegangen. Ich musste es nach Hause schieben.
maɪn ˈfaːɐ̯ʁaːt ɪst ˈlaɪdɐ kaˈpʊtgəˌgaŋən ɪç ˈmʊstə ɛs naːx ˈhaʊzə ˈʃiːbn
my bicycle → unfortunately ← it broke down I I had to it home to push

Unfortunately my bicycle broke down. I had to push it home.

(766) Leider müssen Sie noch etwas warten. – Kein Problem. Das macht mir nichts aus.
ˈlaɪdɐ ˈmʏsn ziː nɔx ˈɛtvas ˈvaʁtn kaɪn pʁoˈbleːm das ˈmaxt miːɐ̯ nɪçts aʊs
unfortunately you have to some more to wait no problem that I don't mind

Unfortunately, you need to wait longer. - No problem. I don't mind.

(767) Es ist immer teurer, während der Schulferien Urlaub zu machen. Das ist die Hochsaison.
ɛs ɪst ˈɪmɐ ˈtɔɪʁɐ ˈvɛːʁənt deːɐ ˈʃuːlfeˌʁiən ˈuːɐ̯laʊp tsuː ˈmaxn das ɪst diː ˈhoːxzɛˌzɔ̃ː
it it is always more expensive during the school holidays to go on vacation this it is the peak season

Vacations during school holidays are always more expensive. This is peak season.

(768) Gemüse wächst in dieser Erde besonders gut.
gəˈmyːzə vɛkst ɪn ˈdiːzɐ ˈeːɐ̯də bəˈzɔndɐs guːt
vegetables it grows in this soil especially well

Vegetables grow especially well in this soil.

(769) Fahrzeugemissionen verschmutzen die Luft.
ˈfaːɐ̯tsɔɪgəmɪˌsioːnən fɛɐ̯ˈʃmʊtsn diː lʊft
vehicle emissions they pollute the air

Vehicle emissions pollute the air.

(770) In dieser Straße sind keine Fahrzeuge erlaubt. Nur Fußgänger.
ɪn ˈdiːzɐ ˈʃtʁaːsə zɪnt ˈkaɪnə ˈfaːɐ̯tsɔɪgə ɛɐ̯ˈlaʊpt nuːɐ ˈfuːsˌgɛŋɐ
on this street they are no vehicles allowed only pedestrians

Vehicles are not allowed on this street. Pedestrians only.

(771) In diesem Land herrscht immer noch Krieg.
ɪn ˈdiːzəm lant hɛʁʃt ˈɪmɐ nɔx kʁiːk
in this country it prevails still war

War is still prevalent in this country.

(772) Händewaschen ist ein guter Schutz vor Krankheiten.
ˈhɛndəˌvaʃn ɪst aɪn ˈguːtɐ ʃʊts foːɐ ˈkʁaŋkˌhaɪtn
hand washing it is a good protection against sickness

Washing hands is good protection against getting sick.

(773) Wir müssen unbedingt wieder auftanken. Wir haben kaum noch Benzin im Tank.
   viːɐ 'mʏsn 'ʊnbədɪŋt 'viːdɐ 'aʊfˌtaŋkn viːɐ 'haːbn kaʊm nɔx bɛn'tsiːn ɪm taŋk
   we we have to absolutely again to fill up we we have hardly any gasoline in the tank

   We absolutely must refuel. We have almost no gas left.

(774) Wir haben uns alle zum Abschied umarmt.
   viːɐ 'haːbn ʊns 'alə tsʊm 'apʃiːt ʊm'aʁmt
   we → all goodbye ←we hugged

   We all hugged as we said goodbye.

(775) Wir gehen nach dem Abendessen immer spazieren.
   viːɐ 'geːən naːx deːm 'aːbntˌɛsn 'ɪmɐ ʃpa'tsiːʁən
   we we go for a walk→ after the dinner always ←

   We always go for a walk after dinner.

(776) Wir sind ungefähr im gleichen Alter.
   viːɐ zɪnt 'ʊngəfɛːɐ ɪm 'glaɪçn 'altɐ
   we we are about in the same age

   We are about the same age.

(777) Wir gehen um Punkt 8 Uhr los. Sei bitte pünktlich.
   viːɐ 'geːən ʊm pʊŋkt axt uːɐ loːs zaɪ 'bɪtə 'pʏŋktlɪç
   we we leave→ at exactly eight o'clock ← be please on time

   We are leaving at 8 o'clock sharp. Please be here on time.

(778) Wir haben jeden Tag außer samstags geöffnet.
   viːɐ 'haːbn 'jeːdn taːk 'aʊsɐ 'zamstaːks gə'œfnət
   we → every day except Saturdays ←we are open

   We are open every day except Saturday.

(779) Wir sitzen im Wohnzimmer und schauen fern.
   viːɐ 'zɪtsn ɪm 'voːnˌtsɪmɐ ʊnt 'ʃaʊən fɛʁn
   we we sit in the living room and we watch TV

   We are sitting in the living room and watching TV.

(780) Wir übernachten in einem Hotel am Meer.
   viːɐ yːbɐ'naxtn ɪn 'aɪnəm ho'tɛl am meːɐ
   we we spend the night in a hotel by the sea

   We are staying at a hotel by the sea.

(781) Wir haben ein Stück Land gekauft und wollen dort ein Haus bauen.
   viːɐ 'haːbn aɪn ʃtʏk lant gə'kaʊft ʊnt 'vɔlən dɔʁt aɪn haʊs 'baʊən
   we → a piece of land ←we bought and we want there a house to build

   We bought a piece of land and want to build a house there.

(782) Wir haben uns eine neue Couch und einen Sessel gekauft.
   viːɐ 'haːbn ʊns 'aɪnə 'nɔɪə kaʊtʃ ʊnt 'aɪnən 'zɛsl gə'kaʊft
   we → ourselves a new couch and an armchair ←we bought

   We bought ourselves a new couch and armchair.

(783) Wir sind so schnell wie möglich gekommen.
   viːɐ zɪnt zoː ʃnɛl viː 'møːklɪç gə'kɔmən
   we → as fast as possible ←we came

   We came as quickly as we could.

(784) **Wir können uns morgen treffen, allerdings habe ich bis zum Nachmittag keine Zeit.**
viːɐ ˈkœnən ʊns ˈmɔʁɡn̩ ˈtʁɛfn̩ ˈaledɪŋs ˈhaːbə ɪç bɪs tsʊm ˈnaːxmɪˌtaːk ˈkaɪnə tsaɪt
we we can → tomorrow ←to meet however I have I until the afternoon no time

We can meet tomorrow, however I am not free until after noon.

(785) **Wir haben uns über die politische Debatte unterhalten.**
viːɐ ˈhaːbn̩ ʊns ˈyːbɐ diː poˈliːtɪʃə deˈbatə ʊntɐˈhaltn̩
we → about the political debate ←we chatted

We chatted about the political debate.

(786) **Herzlichen Glückwunsch zur Geburt deines Kindes!**
ˈhɛʁtslɪçən ˈɡlʏkˌvʊnʃ tsuːɐ ɡəˈbuːɐt ˈdaɪnəs ˈkɪndəs
hearty congratulations for the birth of your child

We congratulate you on the birth of your child!

(787) **Wir haben beschlossen, uns ein kleineres, kraftstoffsparenderes Auto zu kaufen.**
viːɐ ˈhaːbn̩ bəˈʃlɔsn̩ ʊns aɪn ˈklaɪnəʁəs ˈkʁaftʃtɔfsˌʃpaːʁəndəs ˈaʊto tsuː ˈkaʊfn̩
we we have decided ourselves a smaller more fuel-efficient car to to buy

We decided to buy a smaller, more fuel-efficient car.

(788) **Wir essen kein Fleisch. Wir sind Vegetarier.**
viːɐ ˈɛsn̩ kaɪn flaɪʃ viːɐ zɪnt veɡeˈtaːʁiɐ
we we eat no meat we we are vegetarians

We don't eat meat. We are vegetarian.

(789) **In unserer kleinen Wohnung haben wir nicht genug Platz.**
ɪn ˈʊnzəʁɐ ˈklaɪnən ˈvoːnʊŋ ˈhaːbn̩ viːɐ nɪçt ɡəˈnuːk plats
in our small apartment we have we not enough space

We don't have enough space in our small apartment.

(790) **Wir haben 1990 geheiratet.**
viːɐ ˈhaːbn̩ ˈnɔɪntseːn ˌhʊndɐtˈnɔɪntsɪç ɡəˈhaɪʁaːtət
we → (in) 1990 ←we got married

We got married in 1990.

(791) **Wir haben einen schönen, großen Gemüsegarten.**
viːɐ ˈhaːbn̩ ˈaɪnən ˈʃøːnən ˈɡʁoːsn̩ ɡəˈmyːzəˌɡaʁtn̩
we we have a nice big vegetable garden

We have a nice, big vegetable garden.

(792) **Wir haben einen Großbildfernseher.**
viːɐ ˈhaːbn̩ ˈaɪnən ˈɡʁoːsˌbɪltˈfɛʁnˌzeːɐ
we we have a big screen TV

We have a TV with a very large screen.

(793) **In dieser Wohnung leben wir seit 2016.**
ɪn ˈdiːzɐ ˈvoːnʊŋ ˈleːbn̩ viːɐ zaɪt tsvaɪˌtaʊzn̩tʊntˈzɛçtseːn
in this apartment we live we since 2016

We have been living in this apartment since 2016.

(794) **Wir haben uns an das Leben in diesem Land gewöhnt.**
viːɐ ˈhaːbn̩ ʊns an daːs ˈleːbn̩ ɪn ˈdiːzəm lant ɡəˈvøːnt
we → the life in this country ←we have gotten used to

We have gotten used to life in this country.

(795) Wir haben gute Plätze – mitten in der vierten Reihe.
viːɐ ˈhaːbn ˈguːtə ˈplɛtsə ˈmɪtn ɪn deːɐ ˈfiːɐtən ˈʁaɪə
we we have good seats in the middle of the fourth row

We have great seats - middle of the fourth row.

(796) Wir haben weder die Zeit noch das Geld für einen Urlaub.
viːɐ ˈhaːbn ˈveːdɐ diː tsaɪt nɔx daːs gɛlt fyːɐ ˈaɪnən ˈuːɐˌlaʊp
we we have neither→ the time ←nor the money for a vacation

We have neither time nor money for vacation.

(797) Wir haben kein Feuerholz mehr.
viːɐ ˈhaːbn kaɪn ˈfɔɪɐˌhɔlts meːɐ
we we have no firewood anymore

We have no more wood for the fire.

(798) Bei uns sind die Maler im Haus, weil wir die Wände
baɪ ʊns zɪnt diː ˈmaːlɐ ɪm haʊs vaɪl viːɐ diː ˈvɛndə
at our place they are the painters in the house because we the walls

neu streichen lassen.
nɔɪ ˈʃtʁaɪçn ˈlasn
to have repainted

We have the painters in the house because we are having the walls repainted.

(799) Dieses Kleid haben wir in vielen verschiedenen Farben.
ˈdiːzəs klaɪt ˈhaːbn viːɐ ɪn ˈfiːlən fɛɐˈʃiːdənən ˈfaʁbən
this dress we have we in several different colors

We have this dress in several different colors.

(800) Wir müssen Sie untersuchen. Es könnte sein, dass Sie
viːɐ ˈmʏsn ziː ʊntɐˈzuːxn ɛs ˈkœntə zaɪn das ziː
we we have to you to examine it it could be that you

innere Verletzungen haben.
ˈɪnəʁə fɛɐˈlɛtsʊŋən ˈhaːbn
internal injuries you have

We have to examine you. It might be that you have internal injuries.

(801) Wir müssen jetzt los, sonst wird es zu spät.
viːɐ ˈmʏsn jɛtst loːs zɔnst vɪʁt ɛs tsuː ʃpɛːt
we we have to now to go otherwise it becomes it too late

We have to go now, otherwise it will be too late.

(802) Wir müssen das Dach reparieren lassen.
viːɐ ˈmʏsn daːs dax ʁepaˈʁiːʁən ˈlasn
we we have to the roof to have it repaired

We have to have the roof repaired.

(803) Wir müssen uns beeilen. Sonst verpassen wir noch
viːɐ ˈmʏsn ʊns bəˈaɪlən zɔnst fɛɐˈpasn viːɐ nɔx
we we have to to hurry otherwise we miss we in the end

den Zug.
deːn tsuːk
the train

We have to hurry. Otherwise we'll miss the train.

(804) Wir müssen sofort Ihren Fuß operieren.
viːɐ ˈmʏsn zoˈfɔʁt ˈiːʁən fuːs opəˈʁiːʁən
we we have to immediately your foot to operate on

We have to operate on your foot immediately.

(805) Wir müssen den Abfall vom wiederverwertbaren Müll trennen.
viːɐ ˈmʏsn deːn ˈapˌfal fɔm ˈviːdɐfɛɐˌvɛːɐtbaːʁən mʏl ˈtʁɛnən
we we have to the garbage from recyclable waste to separate

We have to separate the garbage from the recycling.

(806) Wir haben zu wenig Spieler. Wir brauchen noch einen.
viːɐ ˈhaːbn tsuː ˈveːnɪç ˈʃpiːlɐ viːɐ ˈbʁaʊxn nɔx ˈaɪnən
we we have too few players we we need one more

We have too few players. We need one more.

(807) Wir haben zwei erwachsene Töchter.
viːɐ ˈhaːbn tsvaɪ ɛɐˈvaksənə ˈtœçtɐ
we we have two adult daughters

We have two adult daughters.

(808) Vor unserem Haus stehen zwei Bäume.
foːɐ ˈʊnzəʁəm haʊs ˈʃteːən tsvaɪ ˈbɔɪmə
in front of our house they stand two trees

We have two trees in front of our house.

(809) In unserem Unternehmen herrschen gute Arbeitsbedingungen.
ɪn ˈʊnzəʁəm ʊntɐˈneːmən ˈhɛʁʃn ˈguːtə ˈaʁbaɪtsbəˌdɪŋʊŋən
in our company they prevail good working conditions

We have very good working conditions in our company.

(810) Wir haben uns lange nicht mehr gesehen. – Ja, es ist lange her.
viːɐ ˈhaːbn ʊns ˈlaŋə nɪçt meːɐ ɡəˈzeːən jaː ɛs ɪst ˈlaŋə heːɐ
we → for a long time no longer ←we saw each other yes it it has been a long time

We haven't seen each other for a long time. - Yes, that was really long ago.

(811) Wir haben uns gerade zum Frühstücken hingesetzt.
viːɐ ˈhaːbn ʊns ɡəˈʁaːdə tsʊm ˈfʁyːʃtʏkn ˈhɪnɡəˌzɛtst
we → just for breakfast ←we sat down

We just sat down to eat breakfast.

(812) Wir sind mit zweistündiger Verspätung gelandet.
viːɐ zɪnt mɪt ˈtsvaɪˌʃtʏndɪɡɐ fɛɐˈʃpɛːtʊŋ ɡəˈlandət
we → with two hour delay ←we landed

We landed two hours late.

(813) Wir haben das Licht die ganze Nacht angelassen.
viːɐ ˈhaːbn das lɪçt diː ˈɡantsə naxt ˈanɡəˌlasn
we → the light the whole night ←we left on

We left the light on all night.

(814) Wir mögen sie, weil sie so lustig sind.
viːɐ ˈmøːɡn ziː vaɪl ziː zoː ˈlʊstɪç zɪnt
we we like them because they so funny they are

We like them because they are so funny.

(815) Wir wohnen in einer schönen Gegend.
viːɐ ˈvoːnən ɪn ˈaɪnɐ ˈʃøːnən ˈɡeːɡnt
we we live in a nice neighborhood

We live in a nice neighborhood.

(816) Wir wohnen im ersten Stock und meine Eltern wohnen einen Stock über uns.
We live on the second floor, and my parents live on the floor above us.

(817) Wir leben außerhalb der Stadt.
We live outside of the city.

(818) Wir wohnen oben im 3. Stock.
We live upstairs on the 4th floor.

(819) Wir haben lange im Ausland gelebt, aber jetzt sind wir wieder da.
We lived abroad for a long time, but now we are back.

(820) Wir haben die letzten paar Spiele verloren. Zum Glück haben wir diesmal gewonnen.
We lost the last few games. Thankfully we won this time.

(821) Für dieses Problem brauchen wir eine kreative Lösung, weil die üblichen Lösungen nicht funktionieren.
We need a creative solution to this problem because the standard solutions aren't working.

(822) Wir brauchen noch eine Gabel bitte.
We need another fork, please.

(823) Für deine Geburtstagstorte brauchen wir viele Kerzen. Du bist schon alt.
We need lots of candles for your birthday cake. You are old.

(824) **Wir brauchen folgende Angaben von Ihnen: Name, Adresse, und Geburtsdatum.**
viːɐ ˈbʁaʊxn ˈfɔlɡndə ˈaŋˌɡaːbn fɔn ˈiːnən ˈnaːmə aˈdʁɛsə ʊnt ɡəˈbuːɐtsˌdaːtʊm
we we need following details from you name address and birth date

We need the following details from you: name, address, and date of birth.

(825) **Wir brauchen drei bis vier Wochen für die Renovierung.**
viːɐ ˈbʁaʊxn dʁaɪ bɪs fiːɐ ˈvɔːçən fyːɐ diː ʁenoˈviːʁʊŋ
we we need three to four weeks for the renovation

We need three to four weeks for the renovation.

(826) **Wir haben nur eine kleine Wohnung, aber damit sind wir zufrieden.**
viːɐ ˈhaːbn nuːɐ ˈaɪnə ˈklaɪnə ˈvoːnʊŋ ˈaːbɐ daˈmɪt zɪnt viːɐ tsuˈfʁiːdn
we we have only a small apartment but with it we are we happy

We only have a small apartment, but we are happy with it.

(827) **Die Firma gehört uns beiden. Wir sind Geschäftspartner.**
diː ˈfɪʁma ɡəˈhøːɐt ʊns ˈbaɪdn viːɐ zɪnt ɡəˈʃɛftsˌpaʁtnɐ
the business it belongs to us both we we are business partners

We own the business together. We are partners.

(828) **Wir haben vor, unseren anstehenden Urlaub in Portugal zu verbringen.**
viːɐ ˈhaːbn foːɐ ˈʊnzəʁən ˈanˌʃteːəndn ˈuːɐˌlaʊp ɪn ˈpɔʁtuɡal tsuː fɛɐˈbʁɪŋən
we we plan our upcoming vacation in Portugal to to spend (time)

We plan to go to Portugal for our upcoming vacation.

(829) **Wir wollten eigentlich Freunde besuchen gehen, aber dann sind wir einfach zu Hause geblieben.**
viːɐ ˈvɔltən ˈaɪɡntlɪç ˈfʁɔɪndə bəˈzuːxn ˈɡeːən ˈaːbɐ dan zɪnt viːɐ ˈaɪnfax tsuː ˈhaʊzə ɡəˈbliːbn
we we wanted actually friends to go visit but then → we just home ←we stayed

We really wanted to visit friends, but then we just stayed home.

(830) **Wir haben Ihren Brief vom 3. Januar erhalten.**
viːɐ ˈhaːbn ˈiːʁən bʁiːf fɔm ˈdʁɪtn ˈjanuaːɐ ɛɐˈhaltn
we → your letter from the 3rd January ←we received

We received your letter dated January 3rd.

(831) **Wir haben unseren Urlaub in den Bergen verbracht.**
viːɐ ˈhaːbn ˈʊnzəʁən ˈuːɐˌlaʊp ɪn deːn ˈbɛʁɡn fɛɐˈbʁaːxt
we → our vacation in the mountains ←we spent (time)

We spent our vacation in the mountains.

(832) **Wir müssen noch besprechen, wann genau wir losfahren und was wir mitnehmen.**
viːɐ ˈmʏsn nɔx bəˈʃpʁɛçn van ɡəˈnaʊ viːɐ ˈloːsˌfaːʁən ʊnt vas viːɐ ˈmɪtˌneːmən
we we have to still to discuss when exactly we we leave and what we we take with (us)

We still have to discuss exactly when we're leaving and what we're taking with us.

(833) **Wir haben noch zwanzig Minuten bis zur Abfahrt.**
viːɐ ˈhaːbn nɔx ˈtsvantsɪç miˈnuːtən bɪs tsuːɐ ˈapˌfaːɐt
we we have still twenty minutes until the departure

We still have twenty minutes until departure.

(834) **Wir haben einen Umweg nach Hause genommen.**
viːɐ ˈhaːbn ˈaɪnən ˈʊmˌveːk naːx ˈhaʊzə gəˈnɔmən
we → a long way around home ← we took

We took the long way home.

(835) **Wir können uns leider nicht einigen.**
viːɐ ˈkœnən ʊns ˈlaɪdɐ nɪçt ˈaɪnɪgn
we we can → unfortunately not ← to reach agreement

We unfortunately can't come to an agreement.

(836) **Wir machen gewöhnlich Urlaub im Ausland.**
viːɐ ˈmaxn gəˈvøːnlɪç ˈuːɐˌlaʊp ɪm ˈaʊslant
we we go on vacation → usually ← abroad

We usually go abroad on vacation.

(837) **Wir wollen die Freiheit haben, unsere Gedanken auszusprechen.**
viːɐ ˈvɔlən diː ˈfʁaɪhaɪt ˈhaːbn ˈʊnzəʁə gəˈdaŋkn ˈaʊstsuʃpʁɛçn
we we want the freedom to have our minds to speak out

We want the freedom to speak our minds.

(838) **Wir wollen ein Haus bauen und suchen ein günstiges Grundstück.**
viːɐ ˈvɔlən aɪn haʊs ˈbaʊən ʊnt ˈzuːxn aɪn ˈgʏnstɪgəs ˈgʁʊntʃtʏk
we we want a house to build and we look for a low-priced plot of land

We want to build a house and are looking for a cheap plot of land.

(839) **Wir wollen unserem Lehrer ein Geschenk kaufen. Wer ist dabei?**
viːɐ ˈvɔlən ˈʊnzəʁəm ˈleːʁɐ aɪn gəˈʃɛŋk ˈkaʊfn veːɐ ɪst daˈbaɪ
we we want our teacher a gift to buy who (he) is in

We want to buy our teacher a gift. Who would like to join in?

(840) **Wir wollen dir etwas zum Geburtstag schenken.**
viːɐ ˈvɔlən diːɐ ˈɛtvas tsʊm gəˈbuːɐtsˌtaːk ˈʃɛŋkn
we we want to you some for the birthday to give (as gift)

We want to give you something for your birthday.

(841) **Wir wollen die Nacht im Freien unterm Mond und den Sternen verbringen.**
viːɐ ˈvɔlən diː naxt ɪm ˈfʁaɪən ˈʊntɐm moːnt ʊnt deːn ˈʃtɛʁnən fɛɐˈbʁɪŋən
we we want the night outdoors under the moon and the stars to spend

We want to spend the night outdoors under the moon and stars.

(842) **Als Kinder waren wir befreundet, aber jetzt, wo wir Erwachsene sind, können wir uns nicht leiden.**
als 'kɪndɐ 'vaːʁən viːɐ bəˈfʁɔɪndət 'aːbɐ jɛtst voː viːɐ ɛɐˈvaksənə zɪnt 'kœnən viːɐ ʊns nɪçt 'laɪdn
as children we were we friendly but now where we adults we are we can't stand each other

We were friends as children, but we don't like each other as adults.

(843) **Wir beraten Sie in Rechtsangelegenheiten.**
viːɐ bəˈʁaːtn ziː ɪn 'ʁɛçtsˌaŋəleːɡənhaɪtən
we we advise you in legal matters

We will advise you in legal matters.

(844) **Wir leben in dieser Wohnung für ein Jahr und dann ziehen wir um.**
viːɐ 'leːbn ɪn 'diːzɐ 'voːnʊŋ fyːɐ aɪn jaːɐ ʊnt dan 'tsiːən viːɐ ʊm
we we live in this apartment for a year and then we move→ we ←

We'll live in this apartment for a year and then move somewhere else.

(845) **Wir gehen zelten, also nehmen wir ein Zelt mit.**
viːɐ 'geːən 'tsɛltn 'alzo 'neːmən viːɐ aɪn tsɛlt mɪt
we we go to camp so we take we a tent with (us)

We're going camping, so we're taking a tent with us.

(846) **Wir fahren mit Freunden in den Urlaub. Das sollte Spaß machen.**
viːɐ 'faːʁən mɪt 'fʁɔɪndən ɪn deːn 'uːɐˌlaʊp das 'zɔltə ʃpaːs 'maxn
we we go with friends on the vacation that it should to be fun

We're going on vacation with some friends. It should be fun.

(847) **Wir suchen eine Wohnung in zentraler Lage.**
viːɐ 'zuːxn 'aɪnə 'voːnʊŋ ɪn tsɛn'tʁaːlɐ 'laːɡə
we we look for an apartment in central location

We're looking for an apartment in a central location.

(848) **Wir befinden uns nun auf einer Flughöhe von 10.000 m.**
viːɐ bəˈfɪndn ʊns nuːn aʊf 'aɪnɐ 'fluːkˌhøːə fɔn 'tseːnˌtaʊznt 'meːtɐ
we we find ourselves now at an altitude of 10,000 meters

We're now flying at an altitude of 10,000 m.

(849) **Wir stellen das Bücherregal hier in die Ecke.**
viːɐ 'ʃtɛlən das 'byːçɐʁeˌɡaːl hiːɐ ɪn diː 'ɛkə
we we put the bookcase here in the corner

We're putting the bookcase here in the corner.

(850) **Wir bleiben nur bis morgen.**
viːɐ 'blaɪbn nuːɐ bɪs 'mɔʁɡn
we we stay only until tomorrow

We're staying only until tomorrow.

(851) **Sobald wir oben auf dem Hügel sind, legen wir eine Pause ein.**
zoˈbalt viːɐ 'oːbn aʊf deːm 'hyːɡl zɪnt 'leːɡn viːɐ 'aɪnə 'paʊzə aɪn
once we at the top of the hill we are we take a break→ we ←

We're taking a break once we reach the top of the hill.

(852) Wir fahren mit der Fähre auf die Insel.
viːɐ ˈfaːʁən mɪt deːɐ ˈfɛːʁə aʊf diː ˈɪnzl̩
we we go with the ferry to the island

We're taking a ferry to the island.

(853) Wir besuchen morgen meine Schwiegereltern.
viːɐ bəˈzuːxn̩ ˈmɔʁɡn̩ ˈmaɪnə ˈʃviːɡɐˌɛltɐn
we we visit tomorrow my in-laws

We're visiting my in-laws tomorrow.

(854) Was für ein Zufall, dass wir uns hier treffen.
vas fyːɐ aɪn ˈtsuːfal das viːɐ ʊns hiːɐ ˈtʁɛfn̩
what a coincidence that we → here ← we meet

What a coincidence meeting you here.

(855) Was für ein niedliches Baby!
vas fyːɐ aɪn ˈniːtlɪçəs ˈbeːbi
what a cute baby

What a cute baby!

(856) Was für ein Gewitter! Hast du die Blitze gesehen und
vas fyːɐ aɪn ɡəˈvɪtɐ hast duː diː ˈblɪtsə ɡəˈzeːən ʊnt
what a thunderstorm →→ you the lightning ← you saw and

den Donner gehört?
deːn ˈdɔnɐ ɡəˈhøːɐt
the thunder ← you heard

What a thunderstorm! Did you see the lightning and hear the thunder?

(857) Worüber lachst du denn?
voˈʁyːbɐ laxst duː dɛn
what about you laugh you !

What are you laughing at?

(858) Wie hoch sind Ihre monatlichen Ausgaben?
viː hoːx zɪnt ˈiːʁə ˈmoːnatlɪçən ˈaʊsɡaːbən
how high they are your monthly expenses

What are your monthly expenses?

(859) Welche Farbe ist gerade in Mode?
ˈvɛlçə ˈfaʁbə ɪst ɡəˈʁaːdə ɪn ˈmoːdə
which color it is right now fashionable

What color is currently fashionable?

(860) Wann muss ich das Buch in der Bibliothek zurückgeben?
van mʊs ɪç das buːx ɪn deːɐ biblioˈteːk tsuˈʁʏkˌɡeːbn̩
when I have to I the book in the library to give back

What day do I have to return the book to the library?

(861) Welcher Tag ist heute?
ˈvɛlçɐ taːk ɪst ˈhɔɪtə
which day it is today

What day is today?

(862) Was hat der Mann gesagt? Ich habe nur die Hälfte
vas hat deːɐ man ɡəˈzaːkt ɪç ˈhaːbə nuːɐ diː ˈhɛlftə
what → the man ← he said I → only half

verstanden.
fɛɐˈʃtandn̩
← I understood

What did the man say? I only understood half.

(863) Was brauchen wir alles für die Party? – Schreib doch eine
vas ˈbʁaʊxn viːɐ ˈaləs fyːɐ diː ˈpaːɐti ʃʁaɪp dɔx ˈaɪnə
what we need we all for the party write ! a

Einkaufsliste.
ˈaɪnkaʊfsˌlɪstə
shopping list

What do we need for the party? – Make a shopping list.

(864) Was machst du beruflich?
vas maxst duː bəˈʁuːflɪç
what you do you professionally

What do you do for a living?

(865) Was willst du zum Geburtstag?
vas vɪlst duː tsʊm ɡəˈbuːɐtsˌtaːk
what you want you for the birthday

What do you want for your birthday?

(866) Was bedeutet dieses Wort? – Schlag es mal im
vas bəˈdɔɪtət ˈdiːzəs vɔʁt ʃlaːk ɛs maːl ɪm
what it means this word look up→ it ! in the

Wörterbuch nach.
ˈvœɐtɐˌbuːx naːx
dictionary ←

What does this word mean? – Look it up in the dictionary.

(867) Wie heißt dieser Fluss?
viː ˈhaɪst ˈdiːzɐ flʊs
how it is called this river

What is the name of this river?

(868) Was ist los? Hast du Schmerzen?
vas ɪst loːs hast duː ˈʃmɛʁtsn̩
what is wrong you have you pains

What is wrong? Are you in pain?

(869) Was ist deine Muttersprache?
vas ɪst ˈdaɪnə ˈmʊtɐˌʃpʁaːxə
what it is your native language

What is your native language?

(870) Wie heißt deine Frau mit Vornamen?
viː ˈhaɪst ˈdaɪnə fʁaʊ mɪt ˈfoːɐˌnaːmən
how she is called your wife with first name

What is your wife's first name?

(871) Wie lautet dein WLAN-Passwort?
viː ˈlaʊtət daɪn ˈveːlaːn-ˈpasˌvɔʁt
what is your wi-fi password

What is your wi-fi password?

(872) Was für ein Auto hast du? – Ich habe keines.
vas fyːɐ aɪn ˈaʊto hast duː ɪç ˈhaːbə ˈkaɪnəs
what kind of car you have you I I have none

What kind of car do you have? – I don't have one.

(873) Was für Musik hörst du gerne?
vas fyːɐ muˈziːk høːɐst duː ˈɡɛʁnə
what kind of music you listen to you gladly

What kind of music do you like to listen to?

(874) Was würdest du an meiner Stelle tun?
vas ˈvʏʁdəst duː an ˈmaɪnɐ ˈʃtɛlə tuːn
what you would you in my position to do

What would you do if you were me?

(875) Wann und wo wurdest du geboren?
van ʊnt voː ˈvʊʁdəst duː ɡəˈboːʁən
when and where → you ←you were born

When and where were you born?

(876) Wann treffen wir uns? – Gegen 10 Uhr. Wäre dir das
van ˈtʁɛfn viːɐ ʊns ˈɡeːɡn tseːn uːɐ ˈvɛːʁə diːɐ das
when we meet around ten o'clock it would be for you that
recht?
ʁɛçt
okay

When are we meeting? - Around 10 o'clock. Is that okay for you?

(877) Wann bekommen wir die Untersuchungsergebnisse?
van bəˈkɔmən viːɐ diː ʊntɐˈzuːxʊŋsɐˌɡeːpnɪsə
when we receive we the test results

When do we find out the result of the (medical) test?

(878) Als Dr. Levi im Urlaub war, ging ich zu seiner
als ˈdɔktoːɐ ˈleviː ɪm ˈuːɐˌlaʊp vaːɐ ɡɪŋ ɪç tsuː ˈzaɪnɐ
when doctor Levi he was on vacation I went I to his
Vertretung.
fɛɐˈtʁeːtʊŋ
substitute

When Dr. Levi was on vacation, I went to the person who was covering for him.

(879) Wenn ich 18 werde, schmeiße ich eine Riesenparty.
vɛn ɪç ˈaxtseːn ˈveːɐdə ˈʃmaɪsə ɪç ˈaɪnə ˈʁiːznˌpaːɐti
when I eighteen I become I throw I a big party

When I turn 18, I'll have a big party.

(880) Als ich 15 war, wollte ich unbedingt Klavier lernen.
als ɪç ˈfʏnftseːn vaːɐ ˈvɔltə ɪç ˈʊnbədɪŋt klaˈviːɐ ˈlɛʁnən
when I 15 I was I wanted I desperately piano to learn
Aber damals hatte ich kein Geld dafür.
ˈaːbɐ ˈdaːmaːls ˈhatə ɪç kaɪn ɡɛlt daˈfyːɐ
but back then I had I no money for it

When I was 15 years old, I really wanted to learn to play piano. But I had no money for it back then.

(881) Wenn ich mit der Arbeit fertig bin, fahre ich nach Hause.
vɛn ɪç mɪt deːɐ ˈaʁbaɪt ˈfɛʁtɪç bɪn ˈfaːʁə ɪç naːx ˈhaʊzə
when I with the work finished I am I go I home

When I'm finished at work, I'm going home.

(882) Wann soll ich kommen? Hast du morgen Abend Zeit?
van zɔl ɪç ˈkɔmən hast duː ˈmɔʁɡn ˈaːbnt tsaɪt
when I should I to come you have you tomorrow evening time

When should I come? Is tomorrow evening okay with you?

(883) Wenn die Kinder groß sind, haben wir mehr Zeit für
vɛn diː ˈkɪndɐ ɡʁoːs zɪnt ˈhaːbn viːɐ meːɐ tsaɪt fyːɐ
when the kids big they are we have we more time for
uns.
ʊns
ourselves

When the kids are grown, we will have more free time again.

(884) Wann hast du deine Familie das letzte Mal gesehen?
van hast duː ˈdaɪnə faˈmiːliə das ˈlɛtstə maːl ɡəˈzeːən
when → you your family the last time ←you saw

When was the last time you saw your family?

(885) **Wann bist du das letzte Mal zum Zahnarzt gegangen?**
van bɪst du: da:s ˈlɛtstə maːl tsʊm ˈtsaːnˌaːɐtst gəˈgaŋən
when → you the last time to the dentist ←you went

When was the last time you went to the dentist?

(886) **Als wir nach Hause kamen, schliefen die Kinder schon**
als viːɐ naːx ˈhaʊzə ˈkaːmən ˈʃliːfn diː ˈkɪndɐ ʃoːn
when we home we arrived they were asleep the kids already

tief und fest.
tiːf ʊnt fɛst
deep and fast

When we got home, the kids were already fast asleep.

(887) **Woher kommst du? – Aus Frankreich.**
voˈheːɐ kɔmst duː aʊs ˈfʁaŋkʁaɪç
from where you come you from France

Where are you from? - From France.

(888) **Wo übernachtest du? – In der Jugendherberge.**
voː yːbɐˈnaxtəst duː ɪn deːɐ ˈjuːgntˌhɛʁbɛʁgə
where you spend the night you in the youth hostel

Where are you spending the night? - At a youth hostel.

(889) **Wo treiben sich deine sogenannten Freunde**
voː ˈtʁaɪbn zɪç ˈdaɪnə ˈzoːgəˌnantn ˈfʁɔɪndə
where they hang around→ your so-called friends

heute Abend rum?
ˈhɔɪtə ˈaːbnt ʁʊm
tonight ←

Where are your so-called friends tonight?

(890) **Wo willst du dich hinsetzen – draußen oder drinnen?**
voː vɪlst duː dɪç ˈhɪnˌzɛtsn ˈdʁaʊsn ˈoːdɐ ˈdʁɪnən
where you want you to sit down outside or inside

Where do you want to sit - outside or inside?

(891) **Wo sind die Toiletten? – Die Treppe rauf und dann**
voː zɪnt diː toaˈlɛtn diː ˈtʁɛpə ʁaʊf ʊnt dan
where they are the toilets the stairs up and then

links.
lɪŋks
left

Where is the toilet? - Go up the stairs and then left.

(892) **Wo auf deinem Computer hast du die Datei gespeichert?**
voː aʊf ˈdaɪnəm kɔmˈpjuːtɐ hast duː diː daˈtaɪ gəˈʃpaɪçɐt
where on your computer → you the file ←you saved

Where on your computer did you save the file?

(893) **Wohin soll ich meine Bewerbung schicken?**
voˈhɪn zɔl ɪç ˈmaɪnə bəˈvɛʁbʊŋ ˈʃɪkn
where I should I my application to send

Where should I send my application?

(894) **Wo willst du dich hinsetzen? Hinten oder vorne?**
voː vɪlst duː dɪç ˈhɪnˌzɛtsn ˈhɪntn ˈoːdɐ ˈfɔʁnə
where you want you to sit down in back or in front

Where would you like to sit? In the back or in front?

(895) **Gegen welche Krankheiten soll ich mich impfen lassen?**
ˈgeːgn ˈvɛlçə ˈkʁaŋkˌhaɪtn zɔl ɪç mɪç ˈɪmpfn ˈlasn
against which diseases I should I to have myself vaccinated

Which diseases should I get vaccinated against?

(896) **Welche Hose ziehst du heute an? – Die hier.**
ˈvɛlçə ˈhoːzə tsiːst duː ˈhɔɪtə an diː hiːɐ
which pants you wear→ you today ← these here

Which pants are you wearing tonight? - These here.

(897) **Welches Hemd steht mir besser?**
ˈvɛlçəs hɛmt ʃteːt miːɐ ˈbɛsɐ
which shirt it suits me better

Which shirt looks better on me?

(898) **Wer soll für dich einspringen, während du im Urlaub bist?**
veːɐ zɔl fyːɐ dɪç ˈaɪnʃpʁɪŋən ˈvɛːʁənt duː ɪm ˈuːɐˌlaʊp bɪst
who he should for you to stand in while you on vacation you are

Who fills in for you when you are on vacation?

(899) **Wer hat die Seite aus dem Buch gerissen?**
veːɐ hat diː ˈzaɪtə aʊs deːm buːx ɡəˈʁɪsn
who → the page out of the book ←he ripped

Who ripped the page out of the book?

(900) **Wer hat dir das Geheimnis verraten?**
veːɐ hat diːɐ daːs ɡəˈhaɪmnɪs fɛɐˈʁaːtən
who → to you the secret ←he revealed

Who told you the secret?

(901) **Wer passt auf die Kinder auf, während wir im Urlaub sind?**
veːɐ past aʊf diː ˈkɪndɐ aʊf ˈvɛːʁənt viːɐ ɪm ˈuːɐˌlaʊp zɪnt
who he looks after→ the children ← while we on vacation we are

Who will take care of the children while we're on vacation?

(902) **Wer ist der Nächste?**
veːɐ ɪst deːɐ ˈnɛːçstə
who he is the next (person)

Who's next in line?

(903) **Wer ist da? – Ich bin's.**
veːɐ ɪst daː ɪç bɪns
who he is there I I am it

Who's there? - It's me.

(904) **Warum bist du einfach nie zufrieden?**
vaˈʁʊm bɪst duː ˈaɪnfax niː tsuˈfʁiːdn
why you are you just never happy

Why are you never happy?

(905) **Warum hast du so eine dünne Jacke an? Draußen ist es kalt.**
vaˈʁʊm hast duː zoː ˈaɪnə ˈdʏnə ˈjakə an ˈdʁaʊsn ɪst ɛs kalt
why you have on→ you such a thin jacket ← outside it is it cold

Why are you only wearing such a light coat? It is cold outside.

(906) **Wieso bist du nicht gekommen? Ich habe extra auf dich gewartet.**
viˈzoː bɪst duː nɪçt gəˈkɔmən ɪç ˈhaːbə ˈɛkstʁa aʊf dɪç gəˈvaʁtət
why → you not ←you came I → specially for you ←I waited

Why didn't you come? I waited specially for you.

(907) **Wieso bist du denn nicht gleich zum Arzt gegangen?**
viˈzoː bɪst duː dɛn nɪçt glaɪç tsʊm aːʁtst gəˈgaŋən
why → you ! not immediately to the doctor ←you went

Why didn't you go to the doctor right away?

(908) **Warum warst du so lange nicht zu erreichen? Warst du krank?**
vaˈʁʊm vaːʁst duː zoː ˈlaŋə nɪçt tsuː ɛʁˈʁaɪçn vaʁst duː kʁaŋk
why → you so long not to ←to be in touch you were you sick

Why have not you been in touch for so long? Have you been ill?

(909) **Wieso kommt der Aufzug nicht? – Du musst erst den Knopf drücken.**
viˈzoː kɔmt deːʁ ˈaʊfˌtsuːk nɪçt duː mʊst eːʁst deːn knɔpf ˈdʁʏkn
why it comes the elevator not you you have to first the button to press

Why isn't the elevator coming? - You have to press the button.

(910) **Wird das lange dauern? – Es kann etwa eine Stunde dauern.**
vɪʁt das ˈlaŋə ˈdaʊɐn ɛs kan ˈɛtva ˈaɪnə ˈʃtʊndə ˈdaʊɐn
it will that to take a long time it it can about an hour to last

Will it take long? - It may take an hour or so.

(911) **Kommst du mit auf einen Spaziergang? – Ich würde ja gerne, aber ich muss arbeiten.**
kɔmst duː mɪt aʊf ˈaɪnən ʃpaˈtsiːɐˌgaŋ ɪç ˈvʏʁdə jaː ˈgɛʁnə ˈaːbɐ ɪç mʊs ˈaʁbaɪtn
you come you with for a walk I I would like to ! gladly but I I have to to work

Will you come for a walk? - I would like to, but I have to work.

(912) **Kannst du mir bitte eine Salatschüssel geben?**
kanst duː miːɐ ˈbɪtə ˈaɪnə zaˈlaːtˌʃʏsl ˈgeːbn
you can you to me please a salad bowl to give

Will you give me a bowl for the salad, please?

(913) **Kannst du mir helfen, den Tisch für die Feier zu dekorieren?**
kanst duː miːɐ ˈhɛlfn deːn tɪʃ fyːɐ diː ˈfaɪɐ tsuː dekoˈʁiːʁən
you can you me to help the table for the party to to decorate

Will you help me to decorate the table for the party?

(914) **Kannst du mir mit der Bewerbung helfen?**
kanst duː miːɐ mɪt deːɐ bəˈvɛʁbʊŋ ˈhɛlfn̩
you can you me with the application to help

Will you help me with my application?

(915) **Könntest du mir bitte noch Batterien für die Kamera mitbringen?**
ˈkœntəst duː miːɐ ˈbɪtə nɔx bataˈʁiːən fyːɐ diː ˈkaməʁa ˈmɪtˌbʁɪŋən
you could you for me please also batteries for the camera to bring with (you)

Will you please bring extra batteries for the camera?

(916) **Schickt ihr mir eine Postkarte, wenn ihr im Urlaub seid?**
ʃɪkt iːɐ miːɐ ˈaɪnə ˈpɔstˌkaʁtə vɛn iːɐ ɪm ˈuːɐˌlaʊp zaɪt
you send you to me a postcard when you on vacation you are

Will you send me a postcard while you're on vacation?

(917) **Dieser Winter war kälter als sonst.**
ˈdiːzɐ ˈvɪntɐ vaːɐ ˈkɛltɐ als zɔnst
this winter it was colder than usual

Winter was colder than normal.

(918) **Drück mir die Daumen!**
dʁʏk miːɐ diː ˈdaʊmən
cross your fingers for me

Wish me luck!

(919) **Mit einer guten Ausbildung findest du bestimmt einen Job.**
mɪt ˈaɪnɐ ˈguːtən ˈaʊsˌbɪldʊŋ ˈfɪndəst duː bəˈʃtɪmt ˈaɪnən dʒɔp
with a good education you find you surely a job

With a good education you will surely find a job.

(920) **Wer ein höheres Einkommen hat, zahlt mehr Steuern.**
veːɐ aɪn ˈhøːəʁəs ˈaɪnˌkɔmən hat ˈtsaːlt meːɐ ˈʃtɔɪɐn
who a higher income he has he pays more taxes

With a higher income you must pay more taxes.

(921) **Bei Autos muss man regelmäßig den Ölstand prüfen.**
baɪ ˈaʊtos mʊs man ˈʁeːɡlˌmɛːsɪç deːn ˈøːlˌʃtant ˈpʁyːfn̩
with cars one has to one regularly the oil-level to check

With cars you have to check the oil regularly.

(922) **Ohne meine Familie fühle ich mich ein bisschen einsam.**
ˈoːnə ˈmaɪnə faˈmiːliə ˈfyːlə ɪç mɪç aɪn ˈbɪsçən ˈaɪnzaːm
without my family I feel a little lonely

Without my family I feel a little bit lonely.

(923) **Frauen sind in unserem Unternehmen in der Minderheit.**
ˈfʁaʊən zɪnt ɪn ˈʊnzəʁəm ʊntɐˈneːmən ɪn deːɐ ˈmɪndɐhaɪt
women they are in our company in the minority

Women are in the minority in our company.

(924) **Möchtest du ein Ei zum Frühstück?**
ˈmœçtəst duː aɪn aɪ tsʊm ˈfʁyːʃtʏk
you would like you an egg for breakfast

Would you like an egg for breakfast?

(925) **Möchtest du noch etwas zu essen? - Nein, danke. Ich bin satt.**
ˈmœçtəst duː nɔx ˈɛtvas tsuː ˈɛsn̩ naɪn ˈdaŋkə ɪç bɪn zat
you would like you anything else to to eat no thanks I I am full

Would you like anything else to eat? - No thanks, I'm full.

(926) Möchtest du etwas Obst? Ich habe heute gute Birnen.
ˈmœçtəst duː ˈɛtvas oːpst ɪç ˈhaːbə ˈhɔɪtə ˈguːtə ˈbɪʁnən
you would like you some fruit I I have today good pears

Would you like some fruit? The pears are quite nice today.

(927) Würdest du lieber auf dem Land oder in der Stadt leben?
ˈvʏʁdəst duː ˈliːbɐ aʊf deːm lant ˈoːdɐ ɪn deːɐ ʃtat ˈleːbn
you would you rather in the countryside or in the city to live

Would you prefer to live in the countryside or in the city?

(928) Könnten Sie bitte Ihren Namen buchstabieren?
ˈkœntən ziː ˈbɪtə ˈiːʁən ˈnaːmən buːxʃtaˈbiːʁən
you could please your name to spell

Would you spell your name please?

(929) Gestern habe ich Geld auf mein Bankkonto eingezahlt.
ˈɡɛstɐn ˈhaːbə ɪç ɡɛlt aʊf maɪn ˈbaŋkˌkɔntoː ˈaɪnɡəˌtsaːlt
yesterday → I money in my bank account ← I deposited

Yesterday I deposited money in my bank account.

(930) Unser neuer Nachbar hat mit mir gestern im Treppenhaus
ˈʊnzɐ ˈnɔɪɐ ˈnaxˌbaːɐ hat mɪt miːɐ ˈɡɛstɐn ɪm ˈtʁɛpnˌhaʊs
our new neighbor → with me yesterday in the stairwell

geredet.
ɡəˈʁeːdət
← he spoke

Yesterday our new neighbor spoke to me in the stairwell.

(931) Gestern lief im Fernsehen eine Diskussion über das Thema
ˈɡɛstɐn liːf ɪm ˈfɛʁnˌzeːən ˈaɪnə dɪskʊˈsioːn ˈyːbɐ das ˈteːma
yesterday it ran on TV a discussion about the topic of

Einwanderung.
ˈaɪnˌvandəʁʊŋ
immigration

Yesterday there was a discussion on television on the topic of immigration.

(932) Wir haben uns gestern im Wald verlaufen. Erst nach
viːɐ ˈhaːbn ʊns ˈɡɛstɐn ɪm valt fɛɐˈlaʊfn eːɐst naːx
we → yesterday in the forest ← we got lost only after

einer Stunde haben wir den richtigen Weg gefunden.
ˈaɪnɐ ˈʃtʊndə ˈhaːbn viːɐ deːn ˈʁɪçtɪɡən veːk ɡəˈfʊndn
an hour → we the right way ← we found

Yesterday we got lost in the woods. We didn't find the right way until an hour later.

(933) Du musst unbedingt die Bremsen überprüfen lassen.
duː mʊst ˈʊnbədɪŋt diː ˈbʁɛmzn yːbɐˈpʁyːfn ˈlasn
you you must absolutely the brakes to have checked

You absolutely must have the brakes checked.

(934) Für diesen Kurs muss man sich unbedingt im Voraus
fyːɐ ˈdiːzən kʊʁs mʊs man zɪç ˈʊnbədɪŋt ɪm ˈfoːʁaʊs
for this course one must one → absolutely in advance

anmelden.
ˈanˌmɛldn
← to register

You absolutely must register in advance for this course.

(935) **Es ist erlaubt, Gepäck bis zu 20 kg Gewicht mitzunehmen.**
ɛs ɪst ɛɐ̯ˈlaʊpt ɡəˈpɛk bɪs tsuː ˈtsvantsɪç ˈkɪlɔɡram ɡəˈvɪçt ˈmɪttsuˌneːmən
it it is allowed luggage up to 20 kilograms weight to take with (you)

You are allowed to take luggage weighing up to 20 kg.

(936) **Du bist ja auch da! Was für ein Zufall!**
duː bɪst jaː aʊx daː vas fyːɐ̯ aɪn ˈtsuːˌfal
you you are ! also here what a coincidence

You are here too! What a coincidence!

(937) **Du bist bestimmt müde. – Nein, ganz im Gegenteil.**
duː bɪst bəˈʃtɪmt ˈmyːdə naɪn ɡants ɪm ˈɡeːɡntaɪl
you you are surely tired no quite on the contrary

You are surely tired. - No, quite the contrary.

(938) **Da liegst du falsch. Ihre Tochter ist 16, nicht 14.**
daː liːkst duː falʃ ˈiːʁə ˈtɔxtɐ ɪst ˈzɛçtseːn nɪçt ˈfɪʁtseːn
there you are wrong→ you ← their daughter she is sixteen not fourteen

You are wrong. Their daughter is 16, not 14.

(939) **Du kannst das Buch in der Bibliothek ausleihen.**
duː kanst daːs buːx ɪn deːɐ̯ biblioˈteːk ˈaʊsˌlaɪən
you you can the book in the library to borrow

You can borrow the book from the library.

(940) **Ihr Ticket können Sie am Schalter kaufen.**
iːɐ̯ ˈtɪkət ˈkœnən ziː am ˈʃaltɐ ˈkaʊfn
your ticket you can at the counter to buy

You can buy a ticket at the counter.

(941) **Du kannst mich jederzeit anrufen.**
duː kanst mɪç ˈjeːdɐˌtsaɪt ˈanˌʁuːfn
you you can me anytime to call

You can call me anytime.

(942) **Ich bin bis 17 Uhr im Büro anzutreffen.**
ɪç bɪn bɪs ˈziːptseːn uːɐ̯ ɪm byˈʁoː ˈantsuˌtʁɛfn
I I am until 5pm in the office to be available

You can catch me in the office until 5pm.

(943) **Sie können die Straße an der Ampel überqueren.**
ziː ˈkœnən diː ˈʃtʁaːsə an deːɐ̯ ˈampl yːbɐˈkveːʁən
you you can the street at the traffic light to cross

You can cross the street there at the traffic light.

(944) **Du kochst definitiv besser als ich.**
duː kɔxst definiˈtiːf ˈbɛsɐ als ɪç
you you cook definitely better than me

You can definitely cook better than me.

(945) **Du kannst die Datei löschen. Ich brauche sie nicht mehr.**
duː kanst diː daˈtaɪ ˈlœʃn ɪç ˈbʁaʊxə ziː nɪçt meːɐ̯
you you can the file to delete I I need it no longer

You can delete the file. I don't need it anymore.

(946) **Du kannst dir eine Zeitung am Kiosk an der Ecke holen.**
du: kanst diːɐ ˈaɪnə ˈtsaɪtʊŋ am ˈkiːɔsk an deːɐ ˈɛkə ˈhoːlən
you you can yourself a newspaper at the kiosk on the corner to pick up

You can get a newspaper at the kiosk on the corner.

(947) **Man kann auf dem Foto fast nichts erkennen. Es ist ja ganz verschwommen.**
man kan aʊf deːm ˈfoːto fast nɪçts ɛɐˈkɛnən ɛs ɪst jaː gants fɛɐˈʃvɔmən
one one can in the photo almost nothing to recognize it it is ! so blurry

You can hardly recognize anything in the photo. It's so blurry.

(948) **Du kannst die Datei öffnen, indem du hier draufklickst.**
duː kanst diː daˈtaɪ ˈœfnən ɪnˈdeːm duː hiːɐ ˈdʀaʊfˌklɪkst
you you can the file to open by you here to click on it

You can open the file by clicking here.

(949) **Sie können per Kreditkarte oder bar zahlen.**
ziː ˈkœnən pɛɐ kʀeˈdiːtˌkaʀtə ˈoːdɐ baːɐ ˈtsaːlən
you you can by credit card or cash to pay

You can pay by credit card or cash.

(950) **Den Apfel kann man nicht mehr essen. Er ist faul.**
deːn ˈapfl̩ kan man nɪçt meːɐ ˈɛsn̩ eːɐ ɪst faʊl
the apple one can one no longer to eat it it is rotten

You can't eat the apple anymore. It is rotten.

(951) **Man kann das Schild aus dieser Distanz nicht lesen.**
man kan daːs ʃɪlt aʊs ˈdiːzɐ dɪsˈtants nɪçt ˈleːzn̩
one one can the sign from this distance not to read

You can't read the sign from this distance.

(952) **Das muss dir nicht peinlich sein. Das passiert vielen.**
das mʊs diːɐ nɪçt ˈpaɪnˌlɪç zaɪn das paˈsiːɐt ˈfiːlən
that you have to yourself not embarrassed to be that it happens to many

You don't have to be embarrassed. That happens to lots of guys.

(953) **Wegen ein paar Regentropfen braucht man keinen Regenschirm.**
ˈveːgn̩ aɪn paːɐ ˈʀeːgn̩ˌtʀɔpfn̩ ˈbʀaʊxt man ˈkaɪnən ˈʀeːgn̩ˌʃɪʀm
because of a few raindrops one needs one not an umbrella

You don't need an umbrella because of a few raindrops.

(954) **Du brauchst keine Angst zu haben. Der Hund tut dir schon nichts.**
duː bʀaʊxst ˈkaɪnə aŋst tsuː ˈhaːbn̩ deːɐ hʊnt tuːt diːɐ ʃoːn nɪçts
you you need no fear to to have the dog it does to you ! nothing

You don't need to be scared. The dog won't hurt you.

(955) Du brauchst dir keine Sorgen um deine Zukunft zu machen. Arbeite hart und alles wird gut.
You don't need to worry about your future. Just work hard and everything will work out.

(956) Sie bekommen zehn Prozent Rabatt.
You get a ten percent discount.

(957) Sie haben mir zu viel Wechselgeld gegeben.
You have given me too much change.

(958) Sie eignen sich sehr gut für diesen Job.
You have good qualifications for this job.

(959) Sie haben mich missverstanden.
You have misunderstood me.

(960) Du hast keinen Grund, dich zu beschweren.
You have no reason to complain.

(961) Du musst auf den Link klicken, um den Artikel lesen zu können.
You have to click the link in order to read the article.

(962) Du musst das so machen und nicht anders.
You have to do it like this, not like that.

(963) Sie müssen sich während der Landung anschnallen.
You have to fasten your seatbelt during landing.

(964) Du musst mehr auf deine Gesundheit achten, anstatt dauernd zu arbeiten.
You have to pay more attention to your health and not just work all the time.

(965) An der Grenze muss man seinen Reisepass vorzeigen.
You have to show your passport at the border.

(966) **Leider hast du meine Frage nicht beantwortet.**
ˈlaɪdɐ hast duː ˈmaɪnə ˈfʁaːgə nɪçt bəˈantvɔʁtət
unfortunately → you my question not ←you have answered

You have unfortunately not answered my question.

(967) **Nach einem heißen Bad fühlt man sich sofort besser.**
naːx ˈaɪnəm ˈhaɪsn̩ baːt ˈfyːlt man zɪç zoˈfɔʁt ˈbɛsɐ
after a hot bath one feels immediately better

You immediately feel much better after a hot bath.

(968) **Du siehst aber toll aus! Zu welchem Friseur gehst du?**
duː ziːst ˈaːbɐ tɔl aʊs tsuː ˈvɛlçəm fʁiˈzøːɐ geːst duː
you you look→ ! great ← to which hairdresser you go you

You look great! Who is your hairdresser?

(969) **Du hast deinen Regenschirm verloren? Dann solltest du im Fundbüro nachfragen.**
duː hast ˈdaɪnən ˈʁeːgnʃɪʁm fɛɐˈloːʁən dan ˈzɔltəst duː
you → your umbrella ←you lost then you should you
ɪm ˈfʊntbyˌʁoː ˈnaːxˌfʁaːgn̩
in the lost-and-found to check with

You lost your umbrella? You should go ask lost-and-found.

(970) **Sie dürfen hier nicht parken, sonst bekommen Sie einen Strafzettel.**
ziː ˈdʏʁfn̩ hiːɐ nɪçt ˈpaʁkn̩ zɔnst bəˈkɔmən ziː ˈaɪnən
you you may here not to park otherwise you get you a
ˈʃtʁaːfˌtsɛtl̩
parking ticket

You may not park here, otherwise you'll get a ticket.

(971) **Du musst dir den Film unbedingt anschauen. Er ist fantastisch.**
duː mʊst diːɐ deːn film ˈʊnbədɪŋt ˈanˌʃaʊən eːɐ ɪst
you you must → the movie absolutely ←to watch it it is
fanˈtastɪʃ
fantastic

You must absolutely watch the movie. It's fantastic.

(972) **Du hast bestimmt Durst. Was möchtest du trinken?**
duː hast bəˈʃtɪmt dʊʁst vas ˈmœçtəst duː ˈtʁɪŋkn̩
you you have surely thirst what you would like you to drink

You must be thirsty. What would you like to drink?

(973) **Sie müssen den Unfall der Versicherung melden.**
ziː ˈmʏsn̩ deːn ˈʊnfal deːɐ fɛɐˈzɪçəʁʊŋ ˈmɛldn̩
you you must the accident to the insurance company to report

You must report the accident to the insurance company.

(974) **Du brauchst gute Schuhe. Der Weg ist steinig.**
duː bʁaʊxst ˈguːtə ˈʃuːə deːɐ vɛk ɪst ˈʃtaɪnɪç
you you need good shoes the path it is rocky

You need good shoes. The path is rocky.

(975) **Hier muss man sich sogar im Sommer warm anziehen.**
hiːɐ mʊs man zɪç zoˈgaːɐ ɪm ˈzɔmɐ vaʁm ˈanˌtsiːən
here one must one → even in the summer warm ←to get dressed

You need warm clothes here even in the summer.

(976) **Man sieht mit den Augen und riecht mit der Nase.**
man ziːt mɪt deːn ˈaʊgən ʊnt ˈʁiːçt mɪt deːɐ ˈnaːzə
one one sees with the eyes and one smells with the nose

You see with your eyes and smell with your nose.

(977) Du solltest die Wunde mit Alkohol reinigen.
du: ˈzɔltəst diː ˈvʊndə mɪt ˈalkohoːl ˈʁaɪnɪɡn̩
you you should the wound with alcohol to clean

You should clean the wound with alcohol.

(978) Sie sollten den Anweisungen Schritt für Schritt folgen,
ziː ˈzɔltən deːn ˈanˌvaɪzʊŋən ʃʁɪt fyːɐ ʃʁɪt ˈfɔlɡn̩
you you should the instructions step-by-step to follow

um die besten Ergebnisse zu erzielen.
ʊm diː ˈbɛstən ɛɐˈɡeːpnɪsə tsuː ɛɐˈtsiːlən
in order to → the best results ← to achieve

You should follow the instructions step by step for the best results.

(979) Gib niemals auf. Es gibt immer Hoffnung.
ɡiːp ˈniːmaːls aʊf ɛs ɡiːpt ˈɪmɐ ˈhɔfnʊŋ
give up → never ← there is always hope

You should never give up. There is always hope.

(980) Man sollte seine Eltern und Freunde nicht belügen.
man ˈzɔltə ˈzaɪnə ˈɛltɐn ʊnt ˈfʁɔʏndə nɪçt bəˈlyːɡn̩
one one should one's parents and friends not to lie to

You shouldn't lie to your parents or friends.

(981) Man sollte in der Öffentlichkeit nicht in der Nase bohren.
man ˈzɔltə ɪn deːɐ ˈœfntlɪçˌkaɪt nɪçt ɪn deːɐ ˈnaːzə ˈboːʁən
one one should in the public not to pick one's nose

You shouldn't pick your nose in public.

(982) Die Maschine kann einfach per Knopfdruck
diː maˈʃiːnə kan ˈaɪnfax pɛɐ ˈknɔpfˌdʁʊk
the machine it can simply by pressing a button

eingeschaltet werden.
ˈaɪnɡəˌʃaltət ˈveːɐdn̩
to be turned on

You turn on the machine by simply pressing a button.

(983) Du hast schon wieder das ganze Warmwasser verbraucht.
duː hast ʃoːn ˈviːdɐ daːs ˈɡantsə ˈvaʁmˌvasɐ fɛɐˈbʁaʊxt
you → yet again the entire hot water ← you used up

You used up all the hot water again.

(984) Du willst deine Wohnung einrichten? Ich helfe dir dabei.
duː vɪlst ˈdaɪnə ˈvoːnʊŋ ˈaɪnˌʁɪçtn̩ ɪç ˈhɛlfə diːɐ daˈbaɪ
you you want your apartment to furnish I I help you with it

Wir können das gemeinsam machen.
viːɐ ˈkœnən daːs ɡəˈmaɪnzaːm ˈmaxn̩
we we can that together to do

You want to decorate your apartment? I'll help you. We can do it together.

(985) Willst du ein Picknick machen? - Das halte ich für eine
vɪlst duː aɪn ˈpɪkˌnɪk ˈmaxn̩ das ˈhaltə ɪç fyːɐ ˈaɪnə
you want you to have a picnic that I consider a

tolle Idee.
ˈtɔlə iˈdeː
great idea

You want to have a picnic? - I think that's a great idea.

(986) Du hattest Glück, dass du dich nicht verletzt hast.
duː ˈhatəst ɡlʏk das duː dɪç nɪçt fɛɐˈlɛtst hast
you you were lucky that you yourself not you hurt

You were lucky that you didn't hurt yourself.

(987) **Unsere Firma wird Ihnen das kaputte Gerät ersetzen.**
ˈʊnzəʁə ˈfɪʁma vɪʁt ˈiːnən daːs kaˈpʊtə gəˈʁɛːt ɐˈzɛtsn̩
our company it will for you the broken device to replace

You will get a replacement from our company for the broken device.

(988) **Dieses Medikament wird Sie 5 Euro kosten.**
ˈdiːzəs medikaˈmɛnt vɪʁt ziː fʏnf ˈɔɪʁo ˈkɔstn̩
this medicine it will you five Euro to cost

You will have to pay five Euro for this medicine.

(989) **Sie werden von uns eine offizielle Einladung erhalten.**
ziː ˈveːɐdn̩ fɔn ʊns ˈaɪnə ɔfiˈtsiɛlə ˈaɪnˌlaːdʊŋ ɐˈhaltn̩
you you will from us an official invitation to receive

You will receive an official invitation from us.

(990) **Sie bekommen Ihr Gehalt zweimal im Monat ausgezahlt.**
ziː bəˈkɔmən iːɐ gəˈhalt ˈtsvaɪmaːl ɪm ˈmoːnat ˈaʊsgəˌtsaːlt
you you get paid→ your pay twice per month ←

You will receive your pay twice per month.

(991) **Die endgültige Entscheidung wird Ihnen in etwa einer Woche mitgeteilt.**
diː ˈɛntgʏltɪgə ɛntˈʃaɪdʊŋ vɪʁt ˈiːnən ɪn ˈɛtva ˈaɪnɐ ˈvɔxə ˈmɪtgəˌtaɪlt
the final decision → you in about a week ←it is communicated

You'll receive the final decision in about a week.

(992) **Diese Webseite ist bei jungen Lesern beliebt.**
ˈdiːzə ˈvɛpˌzaɪtə ɪst baɪ ˈjʊŋən ˈleːzɐn bəˈliːpt
this website it is with young readers popular

Young people like to read this website.

(993) **Deine Wohnung ist sehr gemütlich. Mir gefällt die Einrichtung sehr gut.**
ˈdaɪnə ˈvoːnʊŋ ɪst zeːɐ gəˈmyːtlɪç miːɐ gəˈfɛlt diː ˈaɪnˌʁɪçtʊŋ zeːɐ guːt
your apartment it is very cozy I like the furniture very well

Your apartment is very cozy. I like the furniture very much.

(994) **Du hast Mundgeruch. Putz dir bitte die Zähne.**
duː hast ˈmʊntgəˌʁʊx pʊts diːɐ ˈbɪtə diː ˈtsɛːnə
you you have bad breath brush your teeth→ please ←

Your breath stinks. Please brush your teeth.

(995) **Deine Meinung ist mir sehr wichtig.**
ˈdaɪnə ˈmaɪnʊŋ ɪst miːɐ zeːɐ ˈvɪçtɪç
your opinion it is to me very important

Your opinion is very important to me.

(996) **Du hast ein Loch in der Hose. – Ich weiß, die ist schon sehr alt.**
duː hast aɪn lɔx ɪn deːɐ ˈhoːzə ɪç vaɪs diː ɪst ʃoːn zeːɐ alt
you you have a hole in the pants I I know it it is already very old

Your pants have a hole. - I know, they are really old.

(997) **Dein Telefon klingelt. Willst du nicht abheben?**
daɪn ˈteːləfoːn ˈklɪŋlt vɪlst duː nɪçt ˈapˌheːbn̩
your telephone it rings you want you not to pick up

Your phone is ringing. Aren't you going to answer it?

(998) Dein Lehrer hat dir einen tollen Rat gegeben.
daɪn 'leːʁɐ hat diːɐ 'aɪnən 'tɔlən ʁaːt gə'geːbn
your teacher → to you a great advice ← he gave

Your teacher gave you great advice.

(999) Du hast Recht. Ich habe Unrecht.
duː hast ʁɛçt ɪç 'haːbə 'ʊnˌʁɛçt
you you are right I I am wrong

You're right. I'm wrong.

(1000) Du bist der Einzige, dem ich vertraue.
duː bɪst deːɐ 'aɪntsɪgə deːm ɪç fɛɐ'tʁaʊə
you you are the only person who I I trust

You're the only person that I trust.

www.ingramcontent.com/pod-product-compliance
Lightning Source LLC
Chambersburg PA
CBHW080559090426
42735CB00016B/3291